D1036184

BLACK SPIRITUALITY AND BLACK CONSCIOUSNESS

BLACK SPIRITUALITY AND BLACK CONSCIOUSNESS
SOUL FORCE, CULTURE AND FREEDOM IN THE AFRICAN-AMERICAN EXPERIENCE

CARLYLE FIELDING STEWART, III

Africa World Press, Inc.

P.O. Box 1892
Trenton, NJ 08607

P.O. Box 48
Asmara, ERITREA

Africa World Press, Inc.

P.O. Box 1892
Trenton, NJ 08607

P.O. Box 48
Asmara, ERITREA

Copyright © 1999 Carlyle Fielding Stewart, III

First Printing 1999

Book design: Wanjiku Ngugi
Cover design: Jonathan Gullery

Library of Congress Cataloging-in-Publication Data

Stewart, Carlyle Fielding, 1961-
    Black spirituality and Black consciousness : soul force, culture & freedom in the African-American experience / by Carlyle Fielding Stewart III
        p.   cm.
    Includes bibliographical references and index.
    ISBN 0-86543-662-2 (hardbound). -- ISBN 0-86543-663-0 (pbk.)
    1. Afro-Americans--Religion. 2. Spirituality--United States.
I. Title.
BR563.N4S773 1998
305.896'073--dc21   98-37141
                                                                CIP

Dedication

To Cain Felder, Lewis Baldwin, Vergel Lattimore, Walter Fluker, Anthony Kelley, Carlton Eversely, Arthur Pressley, the late Willie Robinson Smith, and Al Sampson. Spiritual warriors on the battlefield. Our love and truth and justice.

As a matter of principle, the African-American slave experience, like the experience of Lazarus in the text, teaches that true death is death of the spirit that is separated from its infinite ground, and true bondage is bondage of the human spirit when it is not free to manifest and demonstrate deeds and works of infinite spiritual potential. That is to say, there is no loss of freedom like the loss of infinite spiritual potential, and there is no life of unfreedom like a life where one is unable to consistently manifest and demonstrate deeds and works of infinite spiritual freedom.

—Hycel B. Taylor, II

Contents

Chapter Five

Chapter Six

Chapter Seven

Acknowledgements

My deepest and grateful appreciation to my Executive Administrative Assistant, Ms. Ruth Johnson, who labored diligently to get this manuscript into a final typed draft, and Mrs. Florence Richardson and Ms. Takeshia Gainer, who helped proofread this manuscript for publication. Special thanks to, my good friend and soldier in Christ, Dr. Cain Hope Felder, whose friendship, constant support, and encouragement have been a blessing to me, and Dr. Lewis V. Baldwin, colleague and friend whose scholarship and friendship throughout the years have been an inspiration to me.

Foreword

African-Americans have long expressed their yearnings for freedom through cultural creativity and an engagement with the life and power of the spirit. This is the essential point coursing through this rich and thought-provoking book. Building on his earlier work, *Soul Survivors: An African-American Spirituality* (1997), Carlyle Fielding Stewart, III constructs a model of freedom that is grounded in the cultural and spiritual dimensions of African-American life.

Stewart views African-American spirituality and culture as creative, integrative, and transformative forces that have undergirded the quest for social and political freedom over time. He offers brilliant insights into how African-Americans have employed spirituality and the broader aspects of their culture in creating a liberating ethos or set of values, in expressing the depth of their feelings and worldview, and in resisting the oppressive system that still seeks to dominate, divide, and annihilate them. Here Stewart captures the distinctive features of the black experience while highlighting the significance of spirituality and culture for African-American ethics.

While recognizing an essential unity to African-American life and culture, Stewart remains mindful of the many forms and expressions of black spirituality. Moreover, he acknowledges the role of the church in nurturing the kind of creative soul force and spirituality that shape critical consciousness and inform the processes by which African-Americans interpret and struggle for freedom. The paradigm of freedom Stewart provides should attract wide attention among both. ethicists and theologians who are looking for exciting new directions—for fresh analytical tools, interpretive models, and conceptual frameworks—in the study of culture and spirituality in the African-American context.

Stewart leads the reader carefully into a deeper understanding of the words *Spirituality* and *Culture*, which are defined too narrowly in some circles and too often assumed to need no explication in others. Readers who want to think more intensely about the ethical and theological import of current theories of culture and spirituality have much to learn from this important volume.

—Lewis V. Baldwin
Vanderbilt University
February, 1999

Introduction

This work is a continuing discussion begun in *Soul Survivors: An African-American Spirituality* (1997). In that work, I stated that African-Americans have been soul survivors because African-American spirituality has enabled them to adapt, transcend, and transform the absurdities of racism, oppression, and adverse human conditions into a creative soul culture that has helped them maintain sanity, vitality, and wholeness.

Black spirituality has thus created an ethos where creative and resistant soul force has compelled black Americans to creatively and consistently face and overcome their plight. African-American spiritual praxis has instilled within African-Americans a vitality and determination that resists complete annihilation, dehumanization, and domestication by their adversaries. By creating a context for the creation and expression of black soul culture, African-American spirituality has engendered a model of human freedom that differs from all others. At the heart of this paradigm of freedom is the survival of a people who have been subject to all forms of dehumanization, but who have kept their faith and belief in God, maintained creative and resistant soul force as well as a general reverence for life itself. To be exposed to the cruelest forms of human denigration while maintaining personal dignity, optimism, and an unwavering love of God is a remarkable achievement. It is even more astonishing to experience such cruelty and not harbor lingering hatred for the perpetrators. African-American spirituality has been a powerful force shaping an alternative consciousness, creating both conventional and oppositional modes of behavior and belief that confront, adapt, and ultimately overcome those aspects of the larger culture that have sought their complete subjugation.

In this sequel to *Soul Survivors*, we explore the influence of black spirituality on the formation of black consciousness, black culture, and the black community. We also delineate the role of the black church in modeling and shaping expectations and aspirations of freedom for African-Americans. The fundamental purpose of this project is to posit black spirituality as a functional force for positive transformation in America and to delineate how it has created a context for the practice of cultural and spiritual freedom for African-Americans as they have struggled for sanity, wholeness, and freedom within the American experience.

Influence of Black

Chapter One

A Definition of African-American Spirituality

Creative Soul Force and Resistant Soul Force

Any exploration of African-American freedom must consider the pivotal role of black spirituality in shaping the consciousness, identity, and values of African-American people. The term "spirituality" has a plethora of definitions and descriptions too numerous to enumerate here in their entirety; but for our purposes the term represents the full matrix of beliefs, power, values, and behaviors that shape people's consciousness, understanding, and capacity of themselves in relation to divine reality.

Spirituality is also a process by which people interpret, disclose, formulate, adapt, and innovate reality and their understandings of God within a specific context or culture. It signifies a style or mode of existence, an ethos and mythos that creates its own praxis and culture, and compels identification and resolution of human problems through divine intervention. These processes involve adaptation and transformation of internal as well as external conditions.

To be "spiritual" from an African-American perspective, is to live wholly from the divine soul center of human existence. This center is the core of the universe and the quintessential impetus driving the quest for human fulfillment. Thus, African-American spirituality connotes the possession of a soul force spirit that divinely mediates, informs, and transforms a human being's capacity to create, center, adapt, and transcend the realities of human existence. This creative soul force creates its own culture soul, that is to say, the realm of black existence, where black people discover, analyze, celebrate, valuate, corroborate, and transform the meaning of black life in society. The black culture soul is the oasis of black existence; that orbit of being and behavior where black people freely express and preserve creative soul force while affirming their unique personas as a people.

Two essential elements shape and compel African-American spiritual belief and praxis: *creative soul force and resistant soul force.* Creative soul force has to do with those elements of spirituality that create cultural mechanisms that enable African Americans to adapt, transform, and transcend reality through the creative construction of black culture. Resistant soul force is the power to create, transform, and transcend those barriers and constraints that enforce complete domestication to those values, processes, behaviors, and beliefs that reinforce human devaluation and oppression.

Creative and resistant soul forces are two important elements in African-American spirituality. Creative soul force is the spirit of creativity that forges and fosters culture as a means of constructing and transforming reality. Resistant soul force is the power that thwarts the complete domestication of the spirit for purposes of subjugation, domination, and annihilation.

At the heart of black existence in general, is a movement of the spirit that creates, values, and sustains its own soul force and culture soul. Creative soul force and resistant soul force contain the dynamic spirits of innovation, adaptation, assimilation, and transformation that shape the African-Ameri-

2

can experience and consciousness into positive forces for spiritual and social change.

The culture soul is that constellation or archive of values, beliefs, behaviors, practices, and passions that empower and confer value on African-American life. Soul force is the dynamic impetus for positive change. The culture soul is that regime of value and belief giving permanent sanctity and identity to black life as a positively unique cultural and spiritual entity. Both forces emanate from divine reality and are centered in black people's understanding of themselves primarily as spiritual beings, children of the universe, who are umbilically connected to a God of freedom, liberation, and positive change.

African-American spirituality, then, is unique in that this soul force spirit is the ultimate reference point for black existence. This spirit permeates black life and instills in African-American people a will to survive; a desire to confront and surmount all threats to their being and existence while concurrently creating idioms of life and culture which provide them with adaptive mechanisms that reinforce their sanity, affirm their wholeness, and establish their spiritual and ontological location in American society.

Dona Marimba Richards explains this "soul" as follows:

> The concept "soul" cannot be explained in rationalistic terms. The Western metaphysic is not equipped to discuss it. Soul is the essence of the human in the African view. It is that aspect of the other person that expresses her union with the universal order and through it with all being (Okra, Ka, Se, Emi). It was "soul" that was traumatized by slavery and the sudden imposition of New Europe. It was "soul" that revitalized itself and survived through its connection with the universal African soul. [1]

She employs Leonard Barrett's definition that "soul signifies the moral and emotional fiber of the black man."[2] Barrett states:

3

> Soul force is that power of the Black man that turns sorrow into joy, crying into laughter, defeat into victory. It is patience while suffering, determination while frustrated and hope while in despair. It derives its impetus from the ancestral heritage of Africa, its refinement from the bondage of slavery, and its continuing vitality from the conflict of the present.[3]

This soul force as the sovereign impetus of African-American spirituality is the ultimate adjudicating, corroborating, and legitimating power of African-American life. Thus, African-Americans have a unique spiritual way of being, a spiritual "personality," which is part of their reality and identity. Black life involves the revelation, cultivation, and perpetuation of creative soul force and resistant soul force as dynamics for liberation and positive change. Black Americans are a spiritual people of soul. Their cultural ethos is replete with manifestations of the divine presence. Whether it is black football players bowing their heads in prayer or doing a triumphal endzone dance after scoring a touchdown, or jazz musicians giving thanks to God before playing a "set," there is affirmation and acknowledgment of God's all-pervasive presence, power, and grace in every aspect of black life.

There is, then, no higher reality superseding the presence, power, and majesty of God. African-Americans thoroughly demonstrate and reference this reality and spirit in their culture, language, and beliefs so that spiritual praxis is incontrovertibly an essential part of their *raison d'être* and behavior in the world. Whether it is the Sunday morning shout, thanking and praising God for life in general, or the way a song is sung, unquenchable belief in a higher spiritual reality whose ultimate source is God and creative soul force is a benchmark of African-American life and culture.

This means that black spirituality undergirds, shapes, and informs the African-American paradigm of freedom. Freedom is not simply an external material goal but a way of life, a

4

mode of consciousness, a style of being, and practice of existence whose hallmark is creativity, soul force, and divine love. Freedom is the way one orientates to the circumstances of life, responds to life's realities, and overcome life's challenges.

Furthermore, this spirituality informs and conditions the processes by which African-Americans interpret, value, integrate, and transform life around them. It is the ground of their existence and the basis of their ontological and spiritual attainment. It is the paramount source of their understanding of freedom in American society. Peter J. Paris' depiction of "spirituality" is also useful in this discussion as he states that "the spirituality of a people refers to the animating and integrating power that constitutes the principal frame of meaning for individual and collective experiences."[4]

Howard Thurman describes spirituality as a "growing edge of hope" that actualizes human potential and sustains conscious awareness of the reality of God. For Thurman, a genuine spiritual encounter with God means increasing the awareness of the self and its capacities, trajectories, strengths, and limitations.[5]

Dona Richards says, "Spirituality in an African context does not mean distant or 'non-human,' and it certainly does not mean 'saintly' or 'pristine.' Spirituality refers to spiritual being, to that which gives life, form, and meaning to physical realities. It is the breath of life." [6] Elsewhere she observes that spirituality is "the apprehension of cosmic interrelationship. The apperception of meaning in existence, and the degree to which one is motivated by meaning." [7]

Let me state that no singular description of African-American spirituality exhausts the full spectrum of definitions. The forms and expressions of spirituality of African-Americans are as diverse as the people themselves. However, since we are using this term in explicating its influences on the practice of human freedom, we can identify some salient characteristics that differentiate it from other models.

The statements offered here provide descriptions of the word "spiritual" or "spirituality" for this project. There are several corollaries that form the basis of our contention of African-American spirituality as the foundation of African-American freedom.

First, God, the creator of spiritual soul force, is the creative, animative, integrative, and transformative center of the universe. God is the creative ground or soul of all being and existence. This divine soul is the cohesive nexus of black existence. It permeates every aspect of black life and is the paramount source of black consciousness and spirituality. It is the centering force of African-American consciousness. It solidifies black identity as a unique anthropological hermeneutic and relocates African being in the totality of the cosmos. The creativity of God is the first cosmic principle that translates into the spirit of humankind as a creative project. This creativity distinguishes humanity from other creatures and is an integral feature of the practice of African-American spirituality and the formation of black culture as principal foundations to human freedom.

Second, African-American spirituality is a socially *functional process* or praxis that creates an ethos and culture by which black people encounter, interpret, adopt, adapt, integrate, transform, and transcend human experience through the creative appropriation of divine spirit for self-empowerment and survival. This ethos constitutes the divine soul, which creates its own idioms and realities that reinforce the power and authenticity of black existence through creative and resistant soul force culminating in the formation of a regime of truth in relation to black culture and black spirituality.

Third, African-American spirituality is a *creative process* and practice by which black people interpret, respond to, shape, and live out their understandings of divine reality and culture in the context of racial, political, and social oppression and life in general. The five primary tenets of African-American spirituality as they issue from the divine soul center as a prac-

6

tice of human freedom are formative, unitive or integrative, corroborative, transformative, and sacralative or consecrative. These five functions constitute the principal tenets of African-American spirituality as a paradigm for human freedom.

Fourth, creativity, adaptations, ritualization, innovation, improvisation, transcendence, and transformation are by-products of African-American spirituality and help create the survival mechanisms of black culture and consciousness. The daily practice of African-American spirituality provides black people with the catalysts to consciousness, identity formation, and destiny both individually and collectively and is manifested in the various forms of black behavior and belief that stand apart as unique ontological and cultural realities.

Fifth, African-American spirituality and African-American culture in dialogue create a matrix of practices and beliefs that informs, inspires, reforms, and transforms the meaning, value, and purpose of African-American existence. These processes are the principal vehicles of black culture and black spirituality and are the essential rubrics of the oral black cultural archive, which not only inform and transform black behavior and belief but also corroborate, value, and legitimate black life in general.

Key words here are "soul," "spirit," "dialogical process," "unitive, formative, and transformative consciousness." Through this divine soul reality and the subsequent formation of the black culture soul, African-Americans live, think, and have their being. Spirituality is the means by which they forge a viable existence through creation of soul culture. It is the alpha and omega of all black spiritual striving.

Before specifying various aspects of African-American spirituality and demonstrating their function in the African-American paradigm of freedom, let us briefly turn our attention to some ideas regarding human freedom that might prove efficacious for this project.

Chapter Two

African Spirituality and Human Freedom

Since the beginning of African life many years ago, God, through nature and spirit, invariably created black people as free beings on earth, and African spiritual belief systems have always confirmed that God alone is the sovereign guarantor of human freedom, not government. Government merely reinforces the freedom already bequeathed through nature and the spirit.

W.E. Abraham contends:

> What a government does in terms of the life of any individual is to place limits on his possibility of action, but as the range of his free action goes, a government does little more than to highlight certain possibilities. This it does most often by assuring that opportunities of such choices are protected and underlined.[1]

John M. Mbiti asserts:

> When people explain the universe as having been cre-
> ated by God, they are automatically looking at the
> universe in a religious way. We can say therefore that
> the African view of the universe is profoundly reli-
> gious .... Because of their basic belief that the uni-
> verse is created and sustained by God, they interpret
> their life's experience from that starting point. The laws
> of nature are regarded as being controlled by God di-
> rectly or through his servants. The morals and insti-
> tutions of society are thought to have been given by
> God, or to be sanctioned ultimately by him. [2]

In African as well as African-American societies there is a
hierarchy of spiritual authority whose axis powers govern life
in those communities. However, because there is a moral order in the universe manifested in the governing institutions of
society, those serving them must dispense harmony, goodness
and justice, according to divine caveat.[3] This view is especially significant in those societies where black people have
been oppressed and have not fully attained social and political
freedoms. The rights and freedoms of human-kind from the
African perspective cosmically coincide with the sovereign
freedom of God. God bequeaths freedom through cosmic
birthright, where nature and spirit create the social imperatives for human freedom. God maintains complete sovereignty,
autonomy, and hegemony in the universe and endows humankind with the spirit of freedom as children of God within the
natural order.

W. E. Abraham differentiates between essentialist and
scientific views of African and European cultures and civili-
zations. The essentialist view, which is paradigmatic of Akan
or African culture and society holds that "there is a constant
element in man which is irreducible and is the essence of being a man. The scientific perspective, representative of European civilization, contends that it is possible to analyze human

material and then rearrange them according to a desired dominant principle."[4]

The Akan or the African perspective holds that humankind is endowed at creation with certain irreducible faculties that cannot be altered by external conditions. It is the faculty of the spirit; where the primordial powers of humans culminate in the active engagement and domination of spirit over matter and ethereal over material realities. At birth humankind is imbued with an indomitable spirit bequeathed by God but realized in nature.

Thus, while social and political freedoms are highly valued by African people, spiritual freedom, or freedom of the soul to "be" and create life and culture beyond and within the larger culture, and freedom to fashion a "hermeneutics of existence" that uniquely preserve their identity and culture is the quintessential freedom for African peoples. Freedom to create and to preserve the inner spiritual self, to cultivate imagination and creativity as idioms of survival, is an important dimension of African ideas of freedom. Freedom, then, is not predicated on external conditions or milieu alone, but on the capacity of individuals to create and to respond to life on sovereign terms according to the spirit of God, the creator. It is this premise that is the key to black wholeness, vitality, and well-being and may be the key to human freedom in general.

Individuals are thus free to create their own world and culture within or beyond a world; free to fashion their own values, beliefs, and behaviors in response to the larger culture and society. This means that while external conditions may preclude social and political freedom, freedom of the spirit and soul compels the formation of alternative realities of existence whose notions of freedom resist complete social subjugation. Freedom to be in relation to God is the first freedom for African peoples, for to be free in relationship with God means that however oppressive external social and political conditions become, the African is never completely unfree, because he is always free to be in relationship with God, who

11

is the essence of freedom and power. This is the penultimate *locus* of African consciousness, identity, and destiny. Freedom to be in relation to God is the primordial freedom of African people because God is the first freedom.

Insofar as African peoples have created a distinctive spiritual culture, which molds consciousness and shapes being in societies where freedom is materially and socially denied, suggests that the preservation of a creative soul force or culture soul is especially important to spiritual cohesion and psychological relocation. Spiritual freedom of the soul is an important aspect of African-American life. Having the capacity to create a world with its own idioms of meaning is a significant dimension of African-American spirituality and culture. Soul force, then, is a vital impetus that incites spiritual freedom amid material and political constraints.

The point here is that African and African-American cosmology embraces the primacy of spiritual freedom, that is freedom to be, freedom to act, and freedom to interpret; freedom to create a culture soul or hermeneutics of existence according to divine imperatives. This freedom to "be" is not preeminently conferred by social and political institutions nor is it governed solely by the material forces of history, although the result of such freedom is the transformation of both the individual and society.

Even in cases of later modern African societies, where social institutions, as a result of white colonial influences, became the ultimate arbiters of political freedom, the dispensation of social justice and human freedom must still coincide with the reality of freedom in African cosmology. Freedom is still a divine inheritance bestowed at creation according to the imperatives of the divine nature and spirit. African cosmology, therefore, is at the heart of all African understandings of freedom. Since the universe is sacred and spiritually constituted and regenerated, and since black people are the created of creation, the idea of freedom has profound cosmological implications for African-American spirituality as a practice of freedom.

Thus, from the African perspective, freedom is spiritually and cosmologically bequeathed or inherited. "Man" as a child of nature and product of creation is born a free being. Spiritual freedom is more intimately bound to cosmic forces and realities and vitally linked to the culture soul of black people, culminating in the freedom to be, to imagine and to create conventional and alternative forms of consciousness and existence and to actualize themselves principally as spiritual entities in harmony with the cosmic and social order. The dehumanization of black people by some white, black, and other people has necessitated the drive for African spiritual and psychological freedom. The recentering of African consciousness cannot occur without the movement of a sovereign spirit and, therefore, the reacclamation of the primacy of the spiritual life is essential to fathoming African-American spirituality as a paradigm of human freedom.

Spiritual and cultural freedom create nuances and hermeneutics of black culture and spiritual existence, that emerge as both conventional and alternative forms of psychospiritual liberation for blacks who are socially and politically oppressed. The internal spiritual forms of freedom that blacks created were largely a liberation rejoinder to all external forms of oppression and dehumanization that colonialism and white racism enforced. This interior model of freedom of spirituality and culture has its foundation in the sovereignty of creator and creation in African spiritual cosmology. Because this modality of freedom is primarily inward and spiritual does not preclude its translation into radical social transformation. Spiritual freedom is the infrastructure to social and political freedom. The soul must be free inwardly to strike outwardly for positive social change.

Perhaps Jean Jacques Rousseau, more than any revolutionary European thinker, was closest to the African concept of freedom when he observed in the opening pages of *The*

Social Contract, that "Man is born free but everywhere he is in chains."[5] Here he touches on the essence of the primordial African idea of freedom; that men and women as children of creation are born free according to divine birthright bequeathed in nature through spirit. With the advent of Western society and those institutions ordained to protect and to dispense the freedoms of its citizens, came the alteration of ideas of natural freedom in the social and political order.[6]

The cosmological bases of African and African-American spirituality helps us to grasp the fundamental ground from which all African ideas of freedom emerge.[7] A significant aspect of African and African-American spiritualities is thus the hegemonic and autonomous ways that God, through nature and spirit, still sovereignly shapes black spiritual freedom in defiance to the tyrannies of non-freedom created by various social and political establishments.

Chapter Three

Spirituality and the Hermeneutics of Freedom

Creativity and Translation

As stated above, one hallmark of African-American spirituality, based on the African cosmological worldview of the universe and creation, is the inherent freedom of black people or all persons as the created of God. The hegemony of God as Creator translates into an autonomy of the created in creation. An umbilical nexus exists between the creator and the created that forms the ultimate basis for black existence and freedom in the universe. Since "man" did not create "man," no man, woman, or society can be the ultimate guarantors of human freedom. Since the spirit and soul of black people are the creative life centers of black existence and the primordial shapers of black culture, consciousness, and being, the spirit of God, which infuses black life with creativity, is the ultimate governor of black existence.

This means that God is the essence of every human concern in African spirituality. God is the quintessential, consummate reality. All that is *is* because of God's creativity in the universe. The creative principle is the principal framework for all reality; the first principle of human existence and consciousness. Creativity is thus at the heart of the human capacity to produce, perpetuate, discern, and transform life. It is the primordial foundation of all African and African-American spiritual cosmology. All revolutionary transformation has at its core the reality of creativity.

> The African world view is 'religious' in that spiritual truths are thought to contain the essence of things.... The universe was created (is continually 'recreated') by divine act. We participate in that act as we perform rituals of imitation of the Creator and aspects of the Creator (Oludamare and the Orisha, Onyame and the Abosom, and so forth). [1]

Because spirituality is a dynamic, cosmic process, the creative and translative propensities of the spirit of God have strong implications for African-American spirituality. The great gift of African-American spirituality is its capacity ritually to translate harsh and brutal realities into idioms, rituals, and hermeneutics that create their own survival mechanisms for human existence. The strength and vitality of black culture and spirituality involve these translation rites and rituals that creatively and systematically enhance every area of black life. These creative and translative powers of the spirit have been the key to black freedom in a racist society. Thus a positive aspect of African-American spirituality is the way it has enabled black people to develop, translate, and ritualize the hazards and adversities of their social condition into some meaningful spiritual culture of survival. The soul essence of this culture has been the capacity to create black existence and belief in response to those oppressive and devaluating realities engendered by the larger culture and society.

16

Black spirituality has thus enabled African Americans, as the despised and rejected, as the devalued outcasts of American society, to *create* a hermeneutics of existence, a soul culture, a living archive of soul force empowering them to interpret, decode, recode, translate, and ritualize social terror, oppression, and adversity into creative and meaningful liturgies of human existence. The manner in which the chaos and brutalities of oppression and racism have been translated and ritualized into black culture are manifested in everything from the spirituals to jazz, from black foodways to black folkways, from the Signifying Monkey to Brer Rabbit. This will to survive and to *create* through spiritual expression and cultural vitality culminates not only in *the formation of a hermeneutics of existence or of a black culture soul but in translation rites and capacities that are essential to black sanity and soul survival in America which are the infrastructures of Africa-American consciousness and spirituality. This creative spirituality is sine qua non, the soul of black culture, and the cornerstone of the African-American model of freedom.* Thus in every dimension of black spirituality creative translation is manifest. They range from the creative and expressive forms of worship in black churches to liturgies of survival enabling black people to squarely face, alter, and transcend their social, political, and human conditions. The ability to translate creatively meaninglessness into a positive, creative soul force for survival is paramount here.

If *creativity* is the power of the spirit to modify or alter material reality through creative soul force according to the presence and power of God, *translation* is the ability to derive a soul language, lexicon, idiom, or ethos of functional and symbolic meaning and value through the reality that has been created. The capacity to transform material reality into spiritual necessities is essential to black survival in an oppressive society. This means that blacks are able to take the chaos and dross of human experience and to translate them spiritually

17

and culturally into alternative modalities and symbols of black life that promote black identity, sanity, and wholeness.

A salient aspect of black culture and spirituality is, therefore, the ability to actualize creative soul force by translating creatively the adversities of material reality into spiritual profundities. The manner in which black people utilize creativity as an emblem of spirituality and culture for survival is particularly important for our discussion of freedom, for it is precisely in this capacity that the fundamental ideas of freedom take on their distinctive characteristics.

Creating and translating constitute the ability, in a sense, dynamically to change, name, define, and develop reality into vital and symbolic systems of meaning that are essential to African and African-American survival. Spirituality then, is not merely an objective to be attained at the end of a long journey; it is also a creative process that has functional value and social import in which the individual simultaneously practices and personifies assumptions, attitudes, behaviors, and beliefs that give direction, purpose, and vitality to life amid nefarious and debilitating circumstances or amid circumstances of life in general. The result is the acceptance, transformation, or transcendence of that reality.

The ability to translate ritually, for survival purposes, the negative and destructive forces of human existence through the creative powers of soul force and encode them into the ritual practices of black spirituality, is not only an emblem of African-American freedom but one of the great geniuses of African-American people. Innovation, improvisation, and accommodation as elements of survival are all fruits of creative spirituality. To take the pain and peril of the black experience and to translate them into a creative soul force or hermeneutic could not have occurred without a profound spiritual belief reaching into the depths of the soul and spirit, thus facilitating gifts for survival indispensable to black existence. Plainly stated, black Americans could not have come to this place in time without God and could not have survived had they not used their spirituality as a creative instrument for individual and collective liberation and survival.

Developing conventional and alternative modes of being and consciousness through the various processes of translation is a creative response to alienation by the larger society. Because blacks were not racially, culturally, and socially accepted, they had to develop creative ways of interpreting, confronting, and transcending their hostile milieu. Spiritual praxis allowed them to achieve this without losing their souls and minds in the doldrums of despair. It has also allowed them to attain a measure of sanity while creating a unique culture of survival that would reinforce black value, purpose, belief, and thus create vital community.

The ability to create, to translate, and to ritualize human existence into power, vitality, and meaning are important aspects of African and African-American spirituality. It is the capacity to adapt and to create, to change and to translate reality according to divine intent.

To act proactively, entrepreneurialize, alter, modify, mutate, and translate reality as a co-intentional subject of his own destiny and not as an object of subjugation is inspired by African American spiritual beliefs.[2] Therefore, a central feature of African-American spirituality is its propensity to create and to translate life into new metaphors and idioms as an alternative to oppressive cultures and societies thus preserving the soul of black people and personifying the creative principle of divine reality in African-American life.

This capacity to change, to translate life ritually into meaningful patterns of existence appears more prominently in the creation of the black culture soul and the utilization of soul force as instruments of positive change. Thus these creative gifts have not always been directed towards altering the social and political order; they have also been channeled into creating culture and community which insinuate them into the larger culture and insulate them from its harsher realties. *This is a fundamental rubric of African-American spiritual freedom.*

19

It is freedom that primarily directs itself into creating modalities of existence and being that both embrace and defy, transform and transcend the larger culture and society for the preservation of the culture soul, identity, and community of African-American people.

In other words, the freedom to create is intimately bound to the freedom to be, and to choose a viable course of action, and so long as black people possess this creative, life-translating ability, they can live essentially and spiritually as free persons. To understand African-American spirituality as a paradigm of freedom we must grasp this fundamental idea. Within the American experience with its harsh racism and multiple forms of domination and devaluation, African-Americans have created a unique culture of value and power whose freedom is expressed in the idioms and axioms of black spiritual belief and praxis.

Spiritual freedom means the capacity to create a culture, world, and ethos wherein the sanctity of identity and the worth of oppressed and devalued persons is highly preserved according to the trajectories of the divine spirit and reality. The subtle nuances and entrepreneurial impulses of spirituality suggests a capacity to adapt and to transcend one's social and human condition.

While spirit and culture are creatively essential to the African-American paradigm of freedom, social, and political freedom are also important elements of black survival. To create, adapt, express, transcend, and translate reality, life, and the human condition into distinct metaphors and cultures of meaning that not only speak to the ultimate concerns of black people but articulate their unique identity as people is a strong element of African-American spirituality and integral to *all forms* of black freedom in America.

Thus we might say that spirituality functions to create a trajectory or culture of being whereby black people retain the creative capacity or freedom to embrace or repudiate the oppressive and virtuous aspects of the larger culture and society.

20

Spiritual freedom provides the psychological, emotional, and cultural resources to create within black people and their community alternative or even conventional modes of consciousness and existence through the spirit, thereby creating wholeness and vitality through divine intervention.

African-American spirituality has not only been a creative survival mechanism for black people in America, it has also spawned a culture of belief; a style of existence that shapes an alternative transcendent consciousness, resisting complete domestication and assimilation by racism and oppression. It confers identity and galvanizes black resistance to complete Anglo enculturation and co-aptation. It also inspires the acceptance of those dimensions of Anglo culture that are both positive and beneficial to long-term survival. Herbert Marcuse observed that the great genius of industrial society is its ability to assimilate its opposition.[3] Black spirituality has given African-Americans the capacity to endure and overcome the perils of their plight in America by enabling them to assimilate, translate, and transform the larger culture for survival purposes.

What we mean here is that black spirituality has functioned primarily as an intrinsic, interior psychospiritual cultural force within the very fibers and corpuscles of black being, soul, and consciousness. It has allowed black people to accommodate and to adapt to the larger culture and society while resisting complete amalgamation and annihilation by it. This aspect of black spirituality is important because it has enabled African-Americans to become positively influenced by Anglo and African cultures. This is the *African-American model*. African-Americans are shaped by the forces and realities of Euro-American and African culture. Blacks in America have created a model of culture that blends various Anglo and African realities into a hybrid of functional vitality and survival.

That black spirituality shapes consciousness, grounds being, solidifies identity, and confers meaning, purpose, and

21

vitality *vis-à-vis* repressive, hostile, assimilative, and subjugating opposition is essential to understanding its creative, translative function in "conjuring" or creating culture to use Theophus Smith's term.[4]

The freedom to create systems of literal and symbolic meaning and being, to fashion an ethos that sanctions the creation of conventional and alternative modes of consciousness and being, and thus translate pain into power in an oppressive society is one of the first fruits of African-American spirituality.

To understand the African-American model of freedom, we must fathom how spirituality has relegated the power to create and to re-create black being and meaning in the present and historical context. Thus, the creative and translative capacities of African and African-American spirituality are extremely important in grasping the fundamental reasons why blacks still exist after centuries of oppression, and why blacks can still write, pray, laugh, resist, signify, or transform a world that has incessantly tried to devalue, denigrate, and ultimately destroy them.

Ritualization

To understand the cultural and translative capacities of black people, it is necessary to grasp how translation rituals or ritualization are also important constructs of African and African-American spirituality. Creatively translating the agonies of life through the divine spirit impacts the development of the individual and community. Ritualization of the creative and translative processes of black culture and spirituality are thus important aspects of the sacralization of black life and demythologization of the culture of white racism and oppression.

For black people ritualization or the creation of translation rituals is a means of stabilizing their existence and ordering the chaos of oppression and racism by providing some routinizing and symbolic ceremonial structures in response to the terrors of life. Through ritualization the unfamiliar becomes familiar; the unknown becomes known; that which alienates and dislocates being and spiritual vitality becomes harmonized and ordered through the ceremonial invocation of the spirit and power of divine reality.

In black worship, conversing with God in Holy Ghost prayers, canticles, chants, and shouts is a means of ritualizing and ordering the uncertainties of black existence. Invocation of the spirit is a means of supplanting and translating the absurd into viable symbiotic systems of meaning and vitality. This has always been one of the great gifts of black spirituality and black culture: the capacity to take the entrails of black life in America and to transform and ritualize them into practices and axioms that create meaning, purpose, and vitality.

Malidome Patrice Somé says, "To ritualize life, we need to learn how to invoke the spirits or things spiritual into our ceremonies."[5]

Dona Marimba Richards also observes:

> A ritual is a happening; an event. It is a moment of eternity in which the right set of circumstances combines to create a transcendental experience....Black life abounds with rituals through which we redefine ourselves as Black life by giving group expression to the African ethos.[6]

The importance of ritual is essential to African-American spirituality and was especially critical in the formative phases of black life and culture in America. The ritual dramas of life carried over into the worship and praise services of slaves on the plantation. These ceremonies not only brought order, relief, and understanding to black suffering but also consistently connected them with divine reality amid the absurdities and atrocities of their existence.

John Blassingame observes: "A syncretism of African and conventional religious beliefs, the praise meeting in the quarters was unique in the United States. While whites might be carried away by religious frenzy at occasional 'awakenings,' slaves had an even intense emotional involvement with their God every week."[7] The weekly gathering for praise and worship helped to establish viable ritual patterns in black communities.

Ritualization is an important aspect of African-American spirituality and religious history, for it has preserved sanity within insane social conditions. Ritual not only helps to preserve order amid change and change amid order, it is also an important determinant in managing the uncertainty of the black condition in America. Ritual has thus provided black Americans with the stability needed to get through the storms and trials of life while anchoring them in divine reality. There is much evidence of the efficacy of ritual in black spirituality, black culture and in black life in general.

Victor Turner affirms the vital function of ritual in creating *communitas* in African societies.[8] Malidome Patrice Somé claims the quintessential value of ritual as vehicles of healing and spiritual well-being in human communities that have been dislocated by the mechanization of culture.[9] Both Turner and Somé see ritual as vital in creating communities of healing and belonging.

Translation rituals are important in African-American spirituality, because they relate to what Monroe Fordham calls "adaptive and expressive needs."[10]

The important aspects of ritual in African-American spiritual belief are not only expressive and adaptive; they are inventive. Ritual is not only a means of simulating and humanizing reality, but also is a means of creating reality through patterns, configurations, and symbols that speak to and help shape the ultimate ground of meaning for black people. The essence of life is to be in harmony with the Creator and the created, so that true and genuine human community may transpire.[11]

Thus, one can observe a sacralizing function of ritual in black life, where the dislocation of the spirit of African-American people is reified within the ritual process. The profanities of human existence that alienate, sequester, and destroy the human spirit are transformed into ritual verities that facilitate the harmonization of human existence. That which is lost is found. That which has been cast away has been reclaimed and revaluated in the creation and practice of spirituality and culture.

The ritual dramas and dynamics of African-American spirituality as expressions of human freedom are clearly evidenced in the black worship services, black preaching, singing, praying, healing, and church life, in black life and culture from the mode of dress to the style of walk and talk. We will discuss this more fully in Chapters Five and Six.

The translation rituals not only create modes of consciousness emblematic of African-American spirituality but also are hermeneutical prisms for the adaptation and survival of black life. The way in which black people create a culture of spirituality, adopt conventional and alternative modes of consciousness and belief in harmony with and contrast to the white society represents the means by which they have developed translation rituals as a hermeneutic for human survival.

In summary, translation is the capacity to transform and create new idioms and nuances of meaning for purposes of sanity, well being, and survival. Ritualization is the process of codifying the structures of belief into stabilizing patterns of human existence. Translation and ritualization are the twin cornerstones of the hermeneutics of African-American spirituality and freedom.

25

Chapter Four

Five Functional Dynamics of African-American Spirituality

Chapter One traced both the African cosmological roots of African-American spirituality and affirmed their importance in delineating the African idea of human freedom. Now, this chapter examines five essential components of African-American spiritual praxis which include the *formation* of black consciousness, black *communitas*, and black culture; the *unification* of self and community; and the *corroboration* of value, meaning, and existence for African-American people and the *transformation* and *consecration* of black life as sacred reality.

As an expression of human freedom African-American spirituality is not merely a collective social goal; it also is a process, a style of existence, a mode of consciousness and being that enabled black Americans to survive amid nefarious and adverse social and spiritual conditions. Black life in America has its own norms, forms, beliefs, structures, and practices that make African-American life and culture a unique form of human existence.

Such realities are a synthesis of Anglo and African cultural realities and have formed themselves into an African-American spirituality that impacts the consciousness, identity, and culture of African-Americans and has been a principal catalyst in black people's maintenance of spiritual vitality and social well being despite their troubles in this land.

Our contention in this work is that African-American spirituality not only shapes consciousness, belief, and the realities and expectations of black life in America; as ritual practice it also lends itself to the formation of a living black cultural archive and hermeneutic which reinforces the positive values and identity formation of African-American people. These five functions have historical and contemporary value. They are not only the catalysts for transformation and transcendence during the perils of slavery, but they continue in that role as black people face adversities in the present context of their American experience.

The Formative Function

African-American Spirituality and
the Formation of Black Consciousness

As spiritual process and praxis, African-American spirituality has positively shaped the mind and spirit of black people in America. African-Americans have developed a consciousness that positively affirms black being and existence in the midst of debilitating psychological conditions. This consciousness emanates from the African Americans understanding of themselves primarily as spiritual beings and has helped them resist and overcome all persistent psychological, physical, and spiritual attempts to annihilate and subjugate them by destroying their sense of self-worth in American society. Black people have been at psychological war against those cognitive forces and realities that have attempted to take away their sense of a positive self.

Since the beginning of their American odyssey, blacks, as a people, have been defined virtually as nonpersons. They have been devalued, vilified, castrated, and murdered by their adversaries. Such persecution over the years has engendered the *psychological, physical,* and even *spiritual dislocation* African-American people. For blacks, therefore, the struggle thus has been to recenter themselves as whole persons amid the debilitating constraints of oppression. Black spirituality has helped black people relocate themselves psychologically and spiritually within a racist society and culture by equipping them with the capacity to transcend its constraints. Black psychological self-relocation has allowed black spirituality to be the center of black consciousness, thus enabling black people to process, confront, and eventually surmount all nemesis to their spiritual and psychological well-being.

In the midst of these heart-wrenching realities, black spirituality has been the catalyst in forming consciousness; to use Garth Baker-Fletcher's definition, as "I am ness," or sense of ontological connectedness to God that repudiates all attempts at black devaluation and destruction.[1]

When some whites labeled blacks as "nonhuman" or "less than human,"[2] black spirituality cultivated in African-Americans as "I am ness" that subverted the negative effects of such psychological dehumanization. Songs, prayers, rebellions, and religious ceremonies all provided African-Americans with the creative prisms for countering their plight. Spirituality created mechanisms and hermeneutics of empowerment that helped them survive the perils of racism and slavery. Music, prayers, preaching, and petitions provided the means for spiritually and culturally transcending the psychological devastation of dehumanization and oppression.

Black spirituality, thus, has had psychological and ontological value in helping African-Americans to define themselves cognitively as persons of infinite and intrinsic worth rather than as abject, sycophantic animals. It is my belief that the creation of black culture and the black culture soul, which we discussed earlier and again will discuss later, is a direct response to attempts at spiritual, psychological, and cultural devaluation of people of African descent. Whatever damage done to blacks is undone by the power of spiritual practice and belief.

A formative function of African-American spirituality, then, is its capacity to empower black people to form *alternative consciousness, community,* and *culture,* which intrinsically establishes itself by refuting all attempts by the larger and inner culture at psychological devaluation and infantilization. By inner culture, I mean those blacks who have been adversely affected by dehumanization and have bought into and supported the devaluation and subrogation of their own people. Black spirituality positively reinforces the value, sanctity, and worth of black life for all time.

Thus, helping black America form and ostensibly express identity, culture, and community in direct opposition to white racism and black self-devaluation has been a significant aspect of African-American spirituality.[3] Black spirituality has thus been indispensable in the positive formation of black consciousness and black identity formation. It has heightened awareness of the black self as a positive self and has empowered that self to develop a self-consciousness that exceeds and repudiates the denigrations of black people by the larger culture.

For example, when whites and blacks *defined* and *devalued* blacks spiritually and psychologically because they were slaves, black spirituality enabled them to see slavery as a description of their human condition rather than as a definition of their personhood. The formative elements of spirituality, which are a strong belief in God, obtaining the tools of spiritual and psychological transcendence in the cultivation of survival skills, the consistent use of prayer and other spiritual modalities, allowed them to create an assumptive world, a grid of consciousness and culture that dispelled the complete negativization of their personhood. Everything done by the larger culture to humiliate and hinder blacks was countered by a positive spirituality that empowered black people to actualize potential notwithstanding adversarial conditions.

In *Black Culture and Black Consciousness*, Lawrence W. Levine underscores the role of black religion in the cultural aspects of black identity formation. The cultivation of culture provides a unique psychological matrix through which the black experience is formed, valued, and interpreted.[4]

Similarly, in his work *Slave Culture*, Sterling Stuckey delineates the African elements of slave cultural formations on plantation life.[5] Spirituality is a prominent theme in the adaptive and expressive dimensions of the slavery experience and was vital to overcoming its impediments.

Thus, black spirituality has always enabled black people to imagine and psychologically create their alternative self; their own world and ethos; form their own identity and culture; and thus, construct a context for the continual valuation and empowerment of black being and belief.[6] Psychological relocation is critical to the formation of black consciousness and an important aspect of identity and cultural formation. As the quintessential expression of individual autonomy and personal spiritual freedom, psychological relocation can neither be ultimately sanctioned nor determined by the larger culture and society. The fact that black people retained a belief in God and a freedom to imagine and create an ethos and world consistent with their own sense of humanity and well being is a vital formative element of African-American spirituality.

Important here is the *formation* of black consciousness, culture, and spirituality, which invariably compels African-Americans to formulate, establish, and construct a unique matrix of human existence that reinforces the positive aspects of black personhood and community. Black spirituality is vital to the development of a culture of creativity and consciousness that facilitates black transformation, adaptation, and survival in America. The practice of African-American spiritual

31

beliefs has historically been critical in helping black Americans meet and exceed the excruciating demands of their human dilemma. For example, the creation and implementation of prayer, music, worship, and other liturgical forms of black spirituality have been indispensable to creating and sustaining corporate black psychological well being and integral to cultivating a cognitive "will to be" in a world that often repressively negates such being as a threat to its own existence.

The fact that African-American people could utilize their spirituality as a means of creating unique consciousness and could use that consciousness to enhance spirituality is an important dialectic of the African-American paradigm of freedom. The freedom to create a unique culture was and is a positive response to the various processes of dehumanization and enculturation militated by white racism, oppression, and black self-devaluation.

Black spirituality has thus formatively influenced the processes of psychological relocation indispensable to the formation of black consciousness as a *sui generis* cultural reality. Without African-American spiritual belief systems, it would have been difficult, if not impossible, for black people to create a culture of spiritual freedom as an outgrowth to their enslavement and dehumanization. That black people could turn to God and cultivate various spiritual *operandi* as a means of psychological and physical survival in a malevolent milieu is a testimony to both the gifts and strengths of black spirituality. That black people would develop an alternative positive self to the negative self promulgated by the larger culture is a gift of black spirituality. Spiritual realities, that is to say, looking at life and human experience primarily through spiritual lenses, have provided African-Americans with a capacity for transcendence; an ability to extend beyond the misfortunes and constraints of their existential condition.

Despite the ravages of their social, political, and economic situations, they have created a culture of spirituality, where innovation and transformation have established unique hermeneutics of freedom. In being wholly spiritual amid decadent, unspiritual material circumstances, black people have been able to defy, even thwart complete psychological destruction by their adversaries. Maintaining spirituality was the last bastion to maintaining black humanity, for if white oppressors and their black cohorts succeeded in killing and coopting the African-American spirit, they would have succeeded in completely domiciling them for the purposes of perpetual subjugation and servitude. Enabling the black self to conceive and think of itself in positive spiritual terms did much to thwart the psychological devastations of slavery, racism, and systemic racial oppression.

African-American Spirituality and the Formation of the Black *Communitas*

Equally significant as the formation of black consciousness is the manner in which African-American spirituality has created a framework for the emergence of the black *communitas*. Earlier we noted Victor Turner's definition of this term as a community of healing and belonging. While it is true that blacks in white America were forced into separate communal enclaves or were residentially set apart because of racism and discrimination, black spirituality functioned as a cohesive factor in the creation and sustenance of those communities. Black spirituality became the banner around which the black community could organize and sustain itself as a positive social aggregate. Spiritual beliefs helped confer value and consolidate black life around common religious ideals whose firm foundation and entrepreneurial character created the coalescing substances that wielded and differentiated black communities as significant cultural entities.

In other words, African-American spirituality has not only allowed blacks to relocate themselves psychologically and spiritually in a white racist culture by establishing a positive alternative self to a debased self thus positively contributing to the formation of black identity and consciousness; but African-American spirituality has equally prompted the formation of the black *communitas* as a unique cultural and social entity. Thus, the earliest religious services of slaves on plantations created an initial context for the actualization and reinforcement of those positive norms that make healthy communities. For the slaves, worship and spiritual services established not only positive rituals and the ethos from which black community norms could be established, they also provided a context of communal formation in which blacks could collectively create and sustain signs and symbols, and articulate their expectations, aspirations, and beliefs both socially and symbolically. No other source or reality provided the context or pretext in which the collective concerns of a people could be positively and normatively expressed as African-American spirituality.

These religious and spiritual concerns articulated in the realm of the social collective inspired black people to convene to preach, fellowship, pray, and sometimes revolt themselves out of the agonies of plantation life. They could unite, forge, and share their common interests in relative safety without arousing too much their masters' suspicion.[7] Religion and worship thus provided the synergy for the formation and simulation of the earliest African-American communities and empowered blacks to shape a culture of response that would allow them to embrace and transcend their existential condition.

Lawrence W. Levine again reminds us that "religion continues to be prized for the justice it created in a world that lacked it."[8] In other words, African Americans' spiritual praxis created the context in which the black community could organize itself, collectively articulate its hopes, dreams and aspirations, and develop those symbols, values, and signs that would provide it meaning and inspire its ultimate liberation. Black spiritual praxis created a safe harbor where the forms and norms of communal empowerment could be practiced and realized without threat to masters and the status quo.

Hence black spirituality not only constitutes the common ground for the formation of *communitas* for black Americans; it also provides the spiritual resources that would help them positively transform their social plight. Praying, preaching, healing, singing, organizing, and cultivating a culture of spirituality, black people created a community where spiritual norms would establish value, help maintain identity, and foster a community solidarity that would always consolidate and reinforce the structural and functional forms of black life. Thus, black spirituality cultivated a unique freedom ranging from the creation and codification of black music as the language of freedom to the methods by which the community was organized socially and symbolically as an instrument of freedom. All this occurred in the formation of *communitas* engendered in part by the African-Americans' need to affirm themselves spiritually within a larger corporate community as they struggled for meaning and vitality within the perils of slavery and dehumanization.

V.P. Franklin observes:

> Within the slave community, freedom and self determination were not tied to some abstract bourgeois notion of individualism, but were defined in terms of the amount of personal control that an individual had over his or her destiny.[9]

Thus, the earliest African-American communities were not only formed around spiritual concerns in response to the agonies of living black in a racist society; they were shaped, valued, and forged through the native practice of spirituality as a force for community consolidation and empowerment. The same is true today in African-American communities throughout America. Spirituality is the vital substance around which the ultimate concerns of the black *communitas* are conceptualized, articulated, and actualized. African-American spirituality remains the organizing and totalizing force of African-American communities, that is, promoting solidarity, unity, and a sense of collective meaning and personhood in American society. It is through black spirituality that blacks primarily view and have formed themselves into a collaborative, cohesive community of creative and resistant soul force.

Spirituality, thus, reinforces the positive formation of black communities. If slavery, with all of its ugliness and brutality tried to destroy the positive formation of black communities on plantations, spirituality functioned as a countervailing force to hold black families and communities together. Thus, black spirituality contributed to the positive formation of black consciousness, identity, and community by creating a place where blacks could nurture and support one another. Belief in God and the cultivation of a strong faith enabled African-Americans to create a unique community in which God and the principles of spirituality would dominate as organizing, sustaining, and normalizing forces for community.

Black spirituality was essential in the development of the black *communitas* in the following ways:

• It created a context for spiritual praxis and development;

• It created a pretext for the perpetual gathering of the black community and the formation of vital ritual practices;

• It created an ethos where normative community values could be actualized, syngerized, and realized under oppressive conditions; and

• It simulated the reality of social freedom through ritual practices and spiritual praxis. The point here is that black spirituality was not only a force for psychological liberation of African Americans, but was a socially organizing force that would create the context for the emergence and perpetuation of black *communitas*.

African-American Spirituality and the Formation of Black Culture

Earlier we discussed a formative function of black spirituality as also being the creation of culture or the black cultural archive of belief that confers value, form, and legitimacy to black life. This culture began in Africa, took root in the earliest slave communities where blacks came together to worship, praise God, lament their plight, and thereafter create idioms of vitality and power that would summarily insulate them from devastations of the larger culture and society. It was here that slaves spun tales, created genres, and a hermeneutics of culture through songs, prayers, sermons, and stories about the deeper meaning of black life in relation to divine reality. Spirituality laid the basic groundwork for the emergence of African-American culture.

Robert Park tells us:

> The unifying element in every cultural complex is, in the language of Clark Wissler, a core of ideas and beliefs, actuating a people and in large measure controlling their career.[10]

The faith of African Americans, therefore, played a central role in early black cultural formations, for it was precisely in the context of the community gathering for praise, worship, and the affirmation of life itself that African-American culture had its distinctive beginnings.[11] Moreover, this is precisely why we contend that African-American culture and spirituality have very strong affinities, and that it is difficult to separate them entirely when discussing their influence on black life in America.

The earliest practices of black spirituality, then, created a milieu that established vital linkages with black culture. As black people prayed and worshiped God, they created culture through the practice of black spirituality and black religion which lead to the development of a unique hermeneutic of existence. Thus, a uniquely black hermeneutics of culture became an integral part of the identity formation of African-American communities and spirituality and remain so even today.

The emergence of African-American culture, then, as a distinct entity originally sprang from the soul of black spirituality. While black spirituality helped create black culture, black culture has helped shape black spirituality. We cannot fully conceive of African-American cultural formations without considering the role of spirituality and soul force in shaping black behavior, consciousness, and community through the cultivation of black cultural hermeneutics.

Ironically, in fathoming the place of African-American spirituality in the formation of black culture we must also consider the culture of freedom emerging from those early slave communities. Not only did convening collectively to worship, praise God, denounce the masters, and to "create culture" develop a communal reference point for solidarity and black consciousness; it also fostered opportunities for cultivating meaningful idioms, rituals, and hermeneutics of survival. Such occasions encouraged blacks to create their own psychological, cultural, and spiritual world. By imagining and creating realities both real and symbolic, blacks transcended and transformed the cruelties of their external social condition. They often achieved this by wedding aspects of Anglo and African culture into systems of meaning and adaptation that ensured their long-term survival.

Thus, while slaves were not free according to the Anglo material social definition of freedom, they inherently created in response to oppression, idioms, and hermeneutics of spirituality and culture which gave them the freedom to believe and create, to construct a unique consciousness, community, and culture that preserved their sanity and identity amid chaos and despair. To create culture and meaning through a free spirituality would give blacks a peculiar kind of cultural freedom, enabling them to "compensate" for physical and social slavery. *While their bodies were not socially free, their minds and spirits were free to imagine, interpret, transform, and create a culture inimical to the tyrannies of slavery and their human predicament.* This culture, through creative and resistant soul force, created an ethos where black sanity, well being, and survival could be achieved, maintained, and enhanced. Black spirituality is essential in black cultural formation because it created a context where Anglo and African cultures could be synthesized into survival hermeneutics, or a fusion of horizons, that positively reinforced black existence and created an ethos where creative and resistant soul force could flourish as a catalyst for transformation; and developed an environment where spiritual freedom could be actualized as a catalyst for personal and social transformation.

Therefore, in this particular context, the practice of spiritually created a hermeneutic of freedom that negated and neutralized in the mind of slaves complete spiritual and psychological decimation. While the slaves were not free to mingle with whites racially or socially, they practiced a transcendent faith that affirmed spiritual freedom as a basis of self-worth and well-being. Such spiritual freedom, the paramount source of black culture culminating in creative and resistant soul force, has helped blacks transcend, translate, and transform the devastation of their condition into a positive soul culture.

Thus complete subjugation by blacks *en masse* could hardly transpire, because the continual practice of faith and freedom ultimately repudiated all attempts at complete psychological and spiritual domestication and devaluation. While many blacks were indeed dehumanized and decimated by the experience of slavery and racism, many blacks were able to rise above its devastations through the practice of spirituality. Black spirituality allowed for the development and emergence of a culture of soul and freedom that would defy all final attempts at complete dehumanization by the larger culture.

The earliest slave communities practiced African-American spirituality, which even today plays a quintessential role in enabling the black oppressed to develop a culture of freedom that has helped blacks survive with their souls intact. It is this spirituality, this capacity to confront, conform, transcend, and translate the realities, insanities, and brutalities of slavery, discrimination, and oppression into a meaningful and cultural hermeneutic of existence that is a hallmark of the African-American spiritual paradigm of freedom. Thus, the manner in which African-American spirituality has sponsored and sculpted African-American culture is essential to fathoming its role in developing patterns and practices that have ensured the long-term survival of black people.

Having assessed African-American spirituality in terms of its definitive role in the formation of black consciousness, identity, the black *communitas*, and black culture, let us now turn our attention to its unitive function.

The Unitive Function of African-American Spirituality

The Individual Self and the Community Self

A primary function of African-American spirituality as a practice of freedom is the unity of self and community into a positive framework for human empowerment. Black spirituality has always been a totalizing and unifying force for African Americans. It has protected blacks from complete insanity, thus enabling the black community to establish normative patterns of psychological, spiritual, and cultural existence that have engendered its long-term survival. The chaos resulting from psychological dismemberment from the larger human community and the uncertainties of a violent existence have all created a sense of psychological, ontological, and relational fragility among African-Americans. The firm belief in God and the practice of faith through creative and resistant soul force has augmented the perpetual struggle to overcome the ravages of mind, body, and spirit that dislocates the self from itself and the larger community.

Black spirituality, then, has from its beginnings operated as a humanizing force, creating enclaves of individual and community solidarity that give African-Americans a sense of communal connection and personal completion. Again such "wholeness" is created by establishing a living relationship with God as an autonomous and liberating force for positive change and development. God's concern for the oppressed and His ultimate hegemony over their lives means that the oppressed themselves can never be wholly defined or determined by their oppressors. This belief in God suggests that whatever happens to black people, God is ultimately in charge and ultimately will give them total liberation from all dehumanizing forces.

The *integrated* self is the self that maintains spiritual stasis and equilibrium amid volatile social conditions. It is the self that seeks harmony, balance, wholeness, and "somebodiness" in the world. It is contrasted with what Naim Akbar calls the *alien or anti self,* and what others call the *original self.*[12]

Conversely, there is the *resilient self* that overcomes hardship and pain, trouble, and death by invariably identifying, embracing, and integrating into systems of meaning and power that ultimately give it value and purpose, creating an ethos of personal belonging. The creation of black culture and black spirituality has helped black people create wholeness and balance in the world that has dislocated them.

African-American spirituality, then, has provided black people with frames of meaning and value that have helped them live wholesome lives by providing vital connections to larger systems of meaning and value that lend vitality and purpose. The *integrated self* is thus connected with a higher transcendent reality (God), with the *vertical or spiritual self* as a valued self and the *horizontal self* in the community with others. Black spirituality provides integration for the self by

41

enabling it to create a meaningful self in response to the dislocation and alienation created by racism and oppression.

Thus, African-American spirituality solidifies self-identity and self-unity, enabling black people to achieve an existence of relative equilibrium and harmony that optimizes their humanity under conditions of extreme dehumanization. It instills in black people a collectivizing soul force that has precluded complete self-obliteration as well as complete decimation by adversaries. The truth of the matter, however, is that spirituality has prevented blacks from completely destroying others and themselves. Self-devaluation and disintegration usually compels self-annihilation and alienation.

Self-unity issues from black soul force, which has ultimately established the black self as something more than a slave, a nigger, or an inferior being but a person of infinite value and worth. It affirms that however brutally one is treated, the transgression occurs without God's approval, because there is a soul center of black existence that will never sanction human denigration and devaluation as a normative course of human interaction. Black spirituality has therefore had a humanizing function in creating black self-unity by giving blacks a higher sense of purpose and value in a world that has intentionally sought to demean and destroy them. Riggins Earl calls this the Gnostic self.[13]

Conversely, it has also been a radicalizing force in integrating the self into whole persons, for there is a holy defiance that seethes in the cauldron of black life which thoroughly resists the docilizing, domesticating influences of those who would enslave them.[14] *While the humanizing elements of black spirituality have enabled blacks to create personal stasis and harmony of the soul, the radicalizing aspects have helped blacks resist complete psychological, spiritual, and physical subjugation by giving voice, power, and transcendence to their ultimate concerns.*

As both a humanizing and a radicalizing force, African-American spirituality has been a catalyst for self-integration so that blacks might live with relative peace and sanity in a racially oppressive society. Since blacks have not historically been able to integrate themselves fully into white America's community of the self as fully integrated beings, spirituality has allowed them to create significant patterns of personal existence that would instead create a community of self that would promote self unity and collective unity among African Americans.

While racism and alienation of blacks in America have threatened to destroy their very souls, soul force and the practice of faith and spirituality have enabled them to live as fully integrated selves within the realm of a culture they have created as their own. The fact that blacks have neither destroyed others or themselves *en masse* is a result of this integrative function of black spirituality. African-American spirituality, thus, has had an important influence in promoting psychological, spiritual, and physical well being among African Americans. Without spirituality blacks could not attain human wholeness. Black spirituality created a balance for a self that was at war with the larger racial self as well as the anti-self that created psychological ambiguity and self-hatred. Without its humanizing and radicalizing functions, blacks would not be able to develop some semblance of spiritual and psychological balance in a culture that has kept them perpetually off-balance.

Because African-American spirituality remains one of the humanizing, radicalizing, and holistic forces in black experience, blacks have practiced a freedom of expression that directly defies the various processes of devaluation and repression of the larger society. This freedom is integral to self-sanity and collective unity. Blacks, therefore, must speak their minds through the soul force which establishes the self as a viable entity in society. This is part of being black in America. It is freedom to interpret, value, express, and construct an existence that reinforces positive norms for self and community.

This freedom to express oneself freely without reserva-

43

tion or restraint is a hallmark of African-American spirituality and is essential to self-unity and wholeness under psychologically repressive conditions. Having thrived under the tyranny of a culture of silence and intimidation, speaking freely to God, to self, and to others is a source of psychological liberation and empowerment. The fact that blacks can say *what* they want in the *way* they want, *when* they want freedom has facilitated such free, creative, unbridled expression of the souls of black folk.

The expressive modalities of black spirituality have thus always fostered a culture of creativity and freedom, which is evidenced in everything from "telling it like it is" to the Sunday morning shout. If slaves could do little about their physical plight, they could verbalize their feelings in various spiritual forms of protest. Thus, black spirituality provided the language of defiance that would help black people maintain self-unity and collective unity amid the constraints of social and racial oppression. Speaking freely either to God, to massa, or to oneself is freedom's antithetical response to psychological and physical repression. To oppress a person and mute his voice leads to a debilitating form of psychological disempowerment and communal dismemberment that fosters dislocation. A response to oppression must ensue that could make for personal wholeness. "Telling it like it is" is vital when not having the freedom to change what socially is. It is precisely under such conditions that African-American spirituality spawned the formation of black culture as a humanistic and radicalizing response to psychological and racial oppression. If one could not speak out directly against massa, one could create other avenues of cultural and spiritual expression that would allow one to realize a measure of spiritual freedom while maintaining vitality. It is also true that many blacks did speak out directly against massa and engaged in numerous slave revolts in defiance to white subjugation. Herbert Aptheker documents these violent uprisings in *American Negro Slave Revolts*.[15] African-American spirituality has always encouraged such freedom of expression as a means of solidifying personal identity and corporate unity.

Thus having the opportunity to express one's feelings soulfully encouraged blacks to function as healthy integrated selves in a society that did not recognize them as whole or as human. Spirituality thus played a key role in sustaining psychological wholeness in a culture of silence under conditions of racism and repression.

Joseph L. White makes the following assertion:

> The African world view begins with a holistic conception of the human condition. There is no mind-body or affective-cognitive dualism. The human organism is conceived as a totality made up of a series of interlocking systems. This total person is simultaneously a feeling, experiencing, sensualizing, sensing and knowing being living in a dynamic, vitalistic world where everything is interrelated and endowed with the supreme force of life.... The ability to stay in touch with the energizing process generated by the uplifting experiences of feeling good, sensuality and joy have enabled black folks to revitalize, keep the faith, keep on keepin' on and keep climbin'.[16]

African-American spirituality has been the quintessential force sustaining, integrating, and energizing blacks in American society. No other entity has held more influence in helping blacks to establish psychological integration and equilibrium under chaotic conditions. One man explained it this way:

> After being beaten down all week on my job, talked about, lied on and everything else by white folks and yes, even my own kind, I can go to church on Sunday, praise God, pray to God, sing some songs, hear great preaching, know that I am a child of God and be refuelled to face the terrors of the coming week.[17]

Black spirituality, thus, has a humanizing and redeeming function in helping black people keep it all together amid the whirlwinds of personal experiences. To pray, praise, shout, sing, and construct and transform social reality according to the entreaties of a spirit-filled culture have been invaluable elements for self-unity and spiritual vitality for blacks in America. Moreover, African-American spirituality has provided an ultimate reference point for meaningful existence, a grid or hermeneutic of consciousness and being that compels black people to actualize themselves as fully integrative beings despite the slings and arrows of their outrageous misfortune. Value, self worth, dignity, humanity, and power are the nascent gifts of African-American spirituality bequeathed to African-American people for the purposes of survival.

An additional aspect of the integrative function of African-American spirituality has provided black people with a *transcendent, spiritual self* that prevents their ultimate dehumanization. The transcendent spiritual self helps blacks maintain vital connections with the soul center, the organizing element of their lives. Soul force issues from God, remains the oasis of black life, and is maintained through an autonomous and intimate relationship with God. This transcendent self has ultimately prevented permanent psychological debilitation and annihilation of black people and gives them the capacity to exceed the barriers and constraints imposed on them. The ability to go beyond the perils of psychological disintegration and bondage is essential to establishing and maintaining the supremely integrated self.

Howard Thurman remembers his mother telling him that no matter what happened to them God would take care of them, and also related that his grandmother's understanding of scripture reminded her that she was a child of God although she had been a slave. This is true for many blacks in America, who, having been defined as "less than" by their adversaries and enemies, were always defined as "more than" by the God of their silent tears.

46

This capacity to transcend and surmount, to exceed the barriers, and to face the restraints of external conditions has been a gift of African-American spirituality to African-American people. The transcendent spiritual or vertical self, therefore, empowers blacks to fashion an integrated self by superseding the racial dogmas, sacrandas, and mythologies that perpetuate black psychological and spiritual enslavement.

Furthermore, creating culture has also helped blacks maintain psychological integration under conditions of oppression. To uniquely cultivate the remnants of culture, be it jazz, blues, or the spirituals, and by both embracing and repudiating the dominant culture, provides a freedom and vitality that fosters human wholeness of the soul. The capacity to create such idioms that embrace and reject the dominant modes of enculturation and belief is power and freedom and has been a critical factor in creating and sustaining self and communal integration in African-American communities. While blacks might not have been given the power and freedom to run the American government and to generate hegemony in the social and political realms, they have had the freedom to create oppositional forms of spirituality, culture, and belief that help them to integrate and to relocate themselves as full and wholesome beings in a racist society.

John Blassingame tells us:

> Having a distinctive culture helped slaves to develop a strong sense of group solidarity. They united to protect themselves from the most oppressive features of slavery and to preserve their self esteem.... The most important aspect of this group identification was that slaves were not solely dependent upon the white man's cultural frames of reference for their ideals and values. As long as the plantation black had cultural norms and ideals, ways of verbalizing aggression, and roles in his life largely free from his master's control, he could preserve some personal autonomy.... The slave's

47

culture boasted self-esteem, courage, and confidence as a defense against personal degradation.[18]

Furthermore, the unique character of the African-American condition is that from their genesis in America they have become, well or ill, influenced by Europe and Africa. The self's propensity for integration and vitality lies precisely in its ability to create idioms and configurations of expression and belief that literally and symbolically coalesce these two strands into a cohesive framework for human existence. The African-Americans' desire to embrace yet repudiate the larger culture is not only an insignia of African-American freedom; it is essential in establishing the black integrative self into America's larger corporate community of selves. The true black self will unify itself on its own cultural and spiritual terms, the enticements and inducements of the larger culture notwithstanding.

In other words, the fact that African Americans can create a viable spirituality and culture that both affirms and defies Anglo culture is an important component for establishing model of freedom. The empowered self is realized not only in the actualization of the self's transcendent capacities *vis-à-vis* racism, oppression, and the general constraints of human existence but in the capacity of the self to express, assert, and exceed itself according to the spiritual and cultural trajectories of black life and thought. The ability of the black self to recreate itself culturally and spiritually and to fashion a unique ethos of belief and spirituality is essential to establishing and maintaining wholesome self-integration in a society that has stripped it of personal prerogatives.

Self-empowerment ensues when black people create their own culture as an oppositional and autonomous response, in part, to white racism and oppression. Rather than destroy themselves and their oppressors through unmitigated rage, such animus is often sublimated into cultural and spiritual inventions that augment the quality of black life. Pray about it. Talk about it. Laugh about it. Write a song about it. Directing that urge into a higher ethereal purpose, however, has been one of the great attributes of African-American peoples. The freedom to create a viable culture in response to oppression is the quintessential freedom made possible through the faithful practice of spirituality.

Within the corporate black community then, black spirituality has created a context for the collective realization of strength and vitality among those transcendent and empowered selves who have united to practice the dynamics of faith. As stated above, it was precisely the practice of spirituality in the corporate realm that allowed black people to collectivize initially their strength and communal solidarity in early slave communities.

Not only did the praxis of spirituality shape the norms and configurations of early black communities; it equally provided a social framework for actualizing their aggregate expectations, aspirations, values, ethics, behaviors, and beliefs. Such are the building blocks of cohesive communities. The extent to which the spiritual praxis grounded and supported realization of these communal concerns created the context for the establishment and culmination of the black transcendent self as a corporately empowered self. Thus, the common denominators of individual and corporate self-realization were made possible through the practice of faith and spirituality. No other medium or idiom has presented the opportunities for the corporate realization of freedom or the individual expression of freedom as black religion, culture, and spirituality.

The ritual and ceremonial practices of African-American spirituality in the earliest slave communities has affirmed this communal affirmation of empowerment and continues to do so in contemporary black churches and communities. The practice of African-American spirituality has not only provided dynamics and outlets for the varying expressions of individual freedom, it has invariably created a normative context in which the collective aspirations for freedom could be summarily actualized.

To practice African-American spirituality individually is to actualize a freedom of personal expression and cultural invention. To practice African-American spirituality collectively is to actualize collective empowerment and corporate intention. In other words, since the praxis of African-American spirituality allows the individual to achieve personal integration and wholeness through transcendence and empowerment in community, it has played a prominent role in actualizing black freedom.

African-American spirituality, in its capacity to confer upon believers this transcendent spiritual self by actualizing the collective empowered self, is thus indispensable in achieving and sustaining individual and corporate unity.

As stated earlier, black spirituality has had both a harmonizing, humanizing, and radicalizing function in helping black people achieve self-unity and wholeness. We have also affirmed that the establishment of transcendent and empowered selves in community is an equally integrative function of African-American spirituality.

While the foregoing is important in explaining the unitive function of African-American spirituality, equally significant is a unity of spirit that facilitates individual and communal integration. The spirit of God and the practice of spirituality in black communities have historically and contemporaneously created a uniform framework of existence from which black people derive ultimate ontological meaning. Blackness is not the only primordial ontological source of existential meaning; the spirit of God permeates every aspect of black life. Blackness, thus, signifies a oneness of spirit; a unity of purpose; a zeal, a vitality, a soul force, and a power that creates and perpetuates its own archives of meaning. Blackness does not mean one dimensional or monolithic, but multi-dimensional and multi-faceted.

In other words, the spirit of God is the ultimate unifying force of black existence, and African-American spiritual praxis continually evokes a *consciousness of an ever-increasing awareness of God's presence and possibilities* whereby black people affirm that spirit as the paramount source of black consciousness and community. People are recognized by their spirit. No other force in black life shapes, defines, delineates, and penetrates the life and soul of black folk as the spirit of God. That spirit is synonymous with black life and culture and distinguishes them in the vast array of other cultural realities.

We stated earlier that black spirituality has not only created a social context for the consolidation of the black community but has also established ethereal incentives for unifying them spiritually. The fact that black people are born of the spirit and are lead, anointed, and are empowered by the spirit is a unifying element of African-American existence. Spiritual acts of praising, thanking and acknowledging God in every sphere of life has historically and contemporaneously created a perennial context for unification of black life.

This oneness of the spirit, however, does not negate the spiritual diversity and heterogeneity of black culture and black belief. It only suggests that African-Americans are virtually unanimous in their acclamation of the divine spirit's primal role in governing, strengthening, and empowering their individual and collective concerns. Without the spirit of God working for and through them, black people could not have come this far. That they have come this far attests to the unifying power of the spirit to collectivize their consciousness into a uniform culture of believers. African-American spirituality, as a practice of human freedom, has encouraged the integration of self and community through these various functions.

The Corroborative Function

Self-Valuation and Self-Determination
African-American spirituality has not only facilitated the formation of black consciousness, community, and culture and unified the black self and the communal self into a meaningful

framework for existence, it as also given value and legitimacy to African-American life. We stated earlier that a perpetual struggle for black people in America is realizing the value of full personhood. To corroborate something is to affirm its inherent value; to grant its legitimacy, validation, and power through the confirmation of those systems of purpose and meaning that reinforce and celebrate its humanity.

An insidious effect of racism and oppression is the manner in which blacks have been denigrated, devaluated, and virtually delegitimized as human beings in American society. A great paradox of the American experience is the way blacks have been defined as "the problem" when in fact they have always been the solution to America's problems. "To be European was to have value, to be African was to be without personal worth." [19]

However repulsive and virulent the institution of slavery, it was the solution to the white man's economic problems in the so-called New World. Every major contribution of black people to America since slavery has been an attempt to resolve critical dilemmas and to hold the nation to its promise of liberty and justice for all.

Whether blacks fought in America's wars, filled America's industrial plants, created and strengthened America's industrial economy, or helped develop the carbon filament for America's electric lighting system, African-Americans have made invaluable contributions to American history.

The paradox has been what Alan Watts termed the "law of reversed effort,"[20] or what Gunnar Myrdal called the "tyranny of expectancy."[21] Having made these significant contributions historically has generated only a modicum of interest for white historians and intellectuals, for to laud the achievements of blacks is to refute the myths of black inferiority and black incompetence and to shake the foundations of white America's racially hegemonic and debilitating mythologies.

The problem has been the systemic devaluation and delegitimization of black life, culture, and existence since slavery. A certain enigmatic schizophrenic pathology exists in American society, where the labors and contributions of black Americans in building the nation are seldom acknowledged or are simply repudiated. It is difficult to recognize the superlative achievements of a former race of slaves when they have been defined as less than human, considered to mentally incompetent, in the words of historian Arnold Toynbee, of making any significant contribution to world civilization.[22] Destroying the myth of black inferiority is problematic to some black and white people because it calls for the reconstruction of new systems of beliefs that reinforce new cognitive configurations. It is easier to hold onto such mythologies rather than change them because change requires a transformation of outlook, values, and orientation on the part of those who created the myths.

Equally problematic is how black life, since its "genesis" in America has been virtually defined and devalued by some white people as illegitimate. The quest of African-Americans has been to attain personal and human value in a society that has devalued them and to establish a place of moral and existential legitimacy in a culture that has presumably vanquished their spirit for self-determination.

Joel Kovel put it this way in the context of racism:

> Racism is not a new phenomenon. Men have long tried to identify themselves not only as individuals but members of social groups; and to set up viable social groups, they have thrust others out. These "others" have been differentiated in various ways, for instance, according to clan, tribe, nation, estate, or class. The forms change, but the process of self-definition is seemingly endless. And all these "others" have one feature in common: they are never quite as good as the self. Some mysterious tag of devaluation is attached to the other person as his essential point of distinction from the group of selves.[23]

53

Throughout the history of African-Americans, the machinations of personal devaluation have been consistently and systematically unleashed upon them to complete their domestication and subjugation. Religion, law, politics, culture, and education have all created their own mechanisms of aversion, delegitimization, and exploitation that have insidiously attempted to destroy and refute African Americans' inherent self-worth. The task for some whites in America has largely been to appropriate those invaluable aspects of the black experience for consumptive and fiscal purposes while denying that blacks have made any positive and valuable contribution to America. This has been the game many whites have shamelessly perpetrated on African Americans since their "genesis" in this country.

Accordingly, these sacred areas of American life have cultivated their own mythologies of denigration, buttressed in part through the institutional dispensation and conservation of values, symbols, and constellations of power that compel a systemic negation of African Americans as persons of inherent worth and power.

Molefi Asante and Paulo Freire each tell us that deculturation leads to devaluation.[24] The latter ultimately means the delegitimization of black personhood in totality. The consistent and pervasive devaluation of black life in America is a principal factor in perpetuating America's racial mythologies and a chief catalyst in the continuation of oppression. While blacks have moved from the plantation to the plant, the cognitive and psychological enslavement continues through the various systems of benign and malignant neglect and those cognitive processes that legitimate racial devaluation as normative. The problem is the development of those cognitive structures and reasoning that are designed to devaluate and delegitimate people of African descent.

My contention is that African-American spirituality has worked as a countervailing influence to the devaluation and delegitimization of African-American peoples. The virulence of these processes resides in the manner in which they physically and psychologically seduce and reduce the capacity of black people to transform and transcend their existential condition. Racial mythologies are psychologically and physically debilitating. Systematically and consistently denying that blacks have value sets the perfidious stage for their cognitive disintegration and dislocation. For African-Americans, one might say that part of the American experience has been one continual attempt to eviscerate self-initiative, to stymie their capacity for self-determination by destroying their ability to interpret, value, define, and transform their existential reality. If such processes of infantilization and devaluation were more flagrant and caustic in slavery, they are more cryptic and subtle today.

Devaluation and delegimitization are thus prologues to stripping a people's self-determination, and African-American spirituality has enabled blacks to counter these various forms of psychological devastation. When black people were scorned, rejected, and annihilated just for being black, their spirituality provided mechanisms which facilitated the practice of a life-affirming and life-sustaining faith. The problem are those processes of reasoning that pass themselves off as legitimate, scientific by the intellectual establishment and whose axioms become "verifiable" proofs. For every negative hurled against African-Americans, spiritual belief and faith in God helped cancel out its devastation. Their legitimization and valuation as persons of worth were thus corroborated by the texts and contexts, the vehicles, canticles, and oracles of African-American life and thought. Thus, such spiritual realities as *reading and preaching scripture, the fellowship and communitas of the black church, the creation of culture through music, tales, literature, narratives, and humor, prayer, worship, sexuality, and the spirit that touched every bleeding black heart,* all added an infinite sense of value and purpose to African-American people. The development of creative and

55

resistant soul force is also important repellents to various devaluational processes.

When the white man defined them as beasts and animals, the black preacher called them children of God, persons of infinite value and worth. When the overseer flayed their flesh with the lash, they were given instruments of healing and through the practice of a transcendent faith and spirituality. Every attempt by the larger culture to reduce and destroy the African-American's ontological value created a correlating value that affirmed them as persons and repudiated their devaluations as persons of worth. If their masters hated them, God unequivocally loved them. If the larger society rejected and despised them, God and the faith community affirmed them.

African-American spirituality has thus provided black people with the means of self-determination, for as long as God is at their side, they retain a personal autonomy wholly indispensable to defining themselves and their reality. The capacity to name, define, construct, and transform reality is a first axiom of self-determination. Physical mobility and material resources may be limited, but the mind and spirit remain free to define and determine the nature of reality and the range of personal responses to it. African-American spirituality has given black people this measure of personal freedom despite physical and material bondage; the capacity to interpret and valuate life on black terms by deciding for oneself what is real, who is real, and that God is still in charge notwithstanding the brutalities and ambiguities of their existential condition. This has an important element in black freedom; the power to name, construct, and transform reality through divine empowerment and awareness.

From its genesis to the present, African-American spirituality has always possessed this fundamental purpose; to corroborate, save, value, and legitimize black existence in face of efforts to destroy, devalue, and delegitimize it.

The preached word of God, the fellowship of believers, the prayers of the saints, the songs and litanies of the hopeful, the loving arms of a caring and nurturing community have been hallmarks of African-American spiritual praxis and has saved many black souls from complete unmitigated obliteration.

The point here is that black spirituality not only imbues black people with the capacity to revalue, corroborate, and legitimize black life under the most horrendous and horrific conditions but gives them the capacity to override and subvert the psychological, material, and physical decimations of white racism and oppression. This means that the cognitive patterns for triumph and survival were constructed and conferred in large measure through the practice of spirituality.

Demythologizing Racial Myths and Dogmas

Cultivating a culture of resistance and opposition to the tyrannizing forms of white racism and mythologies along with the development of transcendent, biblical, and narrative modes of consciousness through spiritual praxis were countervailing influences to the processes of black devaluation and dehumanization. That blacks could practice their spirituality, create unique vehicles of expression while creating a unique culture of soul force is equally powerful. These cognitive processes and their "wings of the spirit" have enabled black people to dispel and deprecate mythologies designed to perpetuate their psychological and physical enslavement. One of the greatest tools of psychological oppression is the creation of mythologies that reinforce their "truths" through the prisms of ethical legitimacy. The creation of moral and ethical valuations that sanction such verities aided the establishment and consolidation of such mythologies. Thus, slavery is correct because slaves are animals, and, as Alfred North Whitehead observes, slavery was a central truth of Western culture, a foundational premise to rationalizing the establishment of ancient societies.[25]

57

African-American spirituality has thus functioned as an instrument of demythologization. White people could never morally justify mistreatment of blacks, because the praxis of black spirituality sought to demythologize the myths that legitimized oppression. The untruths, half-truths, and lies propagated as dogma in mythologies could never consummately take root in the consciousness of all African Americans, because the praxis of spirituality refuted their claims by undermining their credence and moral authority. All pretensions to legitimacy were cast aside through both the praxis of spirituality and the creation of culture that articulated truths and realities that challenged prevailing assumptions. Unfortunately, such methods of human denigration succeeded for some black people who hate and despise their very blackness. They have bought into the devaluative processes that engender self-hatred. Still there are others who have openly defied such denigration.

For example, while the slave was not physically free, the praxis of spirituality created internal avenues of spiritual and cultural freedom through the practice of faith. When labeled inferior, the practice of God through the entreaties of the spirit demolished these nomenclatures. Black spirituality has equipped African-Americans with the moral, spiritual, cultural, psychological, emotional, social, and intellectual capacity to demythologize white racism, white supremacy, and social oppression. Black spirituality repels the demons of white racism and racial debilitating mythology. It corroborates the value and legitimacy of black existence as a bona fide spiritual and moral force in the universe. When white masters used scripture to justify slavery, blacks used scriptures to actualize freedom.

Essentially, what we have through the praxis of African-American spirituality is the creation of systems of value, legitimacy, and belief that clarify and corroborate the intrinsic worth and power of African-American people, thus also establishing an archive of spirituality and culture that undergirds various forms of freedom. The cultural, spiritual, and psychological forms of freedom that black people cultivated in response to physical and material slavery are the legitimate progenitors to social and political freedom. The precursors to social and political freedom for African-Americans are thus cultural and spiritual freedom, the capacity to name, define, and determine those systems of value, belief, and culture that corroborate the power and worth of African-American people. This also means the power to name and construct a reality that ensures long-term survival.

Valuation, Truth, and Power

Paradoxically, the problem for those who were slaves is the tendency to allow adversaries to determine their destiny. Human subjugation cannot transpire, however, without granting the subjugators the power and authority to value or delegitimize one's life. When people have the power to determine what is or is not valuable, what is or is not acceptable and therefore normative, they possess the power to determine a people's personhood and destiny. Although blacks have left the plantation, the struggle for hegemony of the mind and soul remains today.

By creating its own culture of value, creativity, and belief, African-American spiritual praxis resists all peremptory attempts by adversaries at limiting the scope and trajectory of the worth of black being in America. Valuation raises the efficacy of truth and power. He who valuates possesses the power to determine the nature of reality and the destiny of peoples. Gunnar Myrdal says, "Valuations are always implied in our search for truth as in all other purposeful behavior."[26]

Elsewhere Michel Foucault states:

> The important thing here, I believe is that truth isn't outside power, or lacking in power: contrary to a myth whose history and functions would repay further study.... Truth is a thing of the world; it is produced

59

> only by virtue of multiple forms of constraint and induces regular effects of power. Each society has its regime of truth, its "general politics" of truth; that is, the types of discourse which it accepts and functions as true.... truth is to be understood as a system of ordered procedures for the production, regulation, distribution, circulation and operation of statements. Truth is linked in a circular relation with systems of power which produce and sustain it, and to effects of power which it induces and which extends it. A regime of truth.[27]

American myths of white supremacy and black inferiority have created their own constellations of power and "truth" (untruths) that perpetuate the devaluation and denigration of African-American people. Black spirituality supplants the untruth embodied in those systems of devaluation that preclude black ascendancy and empowerment.

Elsewhere Foucault observes, "It's not a matter of emancipating truth from every system of power (which would be a chimera, for truth is already power) but detaching the power of truth from the forms of hegemony, social, economic and cultural, within which it operates at the present time."[28]

The demythologization of racial mythology through the precepts and praxis of black spirituality has helped establish an alternative *loci* of black consciousness and belief that moves black people from oppression to psychological and physical self-determination and liberation. We must not obviate the capacity of black spiritual belief in dispelling the predominant mythologies, for it is precisely the acceptance of such dogmas that creates the psychological enslavement of whites and others who embrace such erroneous ideas.

Affirming such beliefs is dangerous, because it belies and misconstrues notions of freedom. John McCall in his analysis of the colonizer and the colonized puts its this way:

The bond between the colonizer and the colonized is destructive because each one, in a sense, is living out of contact with the real world. Equally important, each is giving up inner freedom. The colonized gives up inner freedom when he plays along with the myth and does not accept responsibility. The colonizer gives up freedom when he continues to distort reality so that he can have these advantages and not feel the guilt that always bubbles at the center of his being.[29]

Early in this work we stated that "nonfreedom" is not something historically bequeathed to oppressed blacks by racist whites in social and political forms. Rather it is also exemplified in the beliefs, mythologies, behaviors, and myopic practices of whites in relation to blacks. We might also affirm that the extent to which blacks have bought into oppressive thoughts and practices is also a form of nonfreedom. Racial myths create spheres of ignorance and bias towards others that are highly homophobic. The systems of valuation promulgating and enshrining these racial mythologies as absolute truth are as psychologically enslaving of white people as they are of blacks. This is why one must be precise in explicating who is free or unfree. Who is more free? The person on the ground or the person holding him down? Joseph Barndt provides a telling description of the types of racial myths:

An enormous list of myths and lies about people of color has been created to control the impressions and perceptions of whites as they relate to people of color.... These myths and lies have been handed down from generation to generation of white people. Such crude myths and lies simply declare that Americans of African descent are inferior, ugly, violent, dirty, oversexed animals. They are also happy, measure to the dissemination and deification of these homophobic racial mythologies lazy, dancing, singing, stupid idiots.... Those who accept these lies believe them to be fundamental truths.[30]

61

Dissemination and deification of these homophobic racial mythologies reinforce their functionalizing as truth. The great value of African-American spirituality, then, is its capacity to verify, clarify, and corroborate black personhood as antithesis to the desolations of racism and oppression. Joel Kovel has done significant work in delineating the pathologies and psychohistory of white racism, and much of his work warrants further study.[31] While these mythologies circumscribe white consciousness and behavior, thus making them unfree in their attitudes and beliefs towards blacks, black spirituality has inoculated many but not all African-Americans from its long-term poisonous effects. However much the myths of black inferiority have been overtly and subliminally disseminated to African-American people, belief in God and the practice of spirituality have enabled them to overcome their thoroughgoing indoctrination. Brandt states:

> Africans in the United States never lost sight of freedom, and proclaimed in their spirituals that their slave masters could "kill the body but not the soul." [32]

Devaluation is not only practiced in the general racial phobias of blacks by whites but also embodied in various cognitive processes. Generally speaking, racist thinking posits not only the racial inferiority of black people but equally affirms their intellectual and cultural subordination. Within the matrix of white racist belief is the notion that anything relating to the masses of blacks is invariably substandard, i.e., below the threshold of normal intelligence. A suspicion of the authenticity and value of black intellectual capacity always lingers in America, where blacks must still prove themselves in every arena except athletics.

Again, John McCall is helpful here:

> When you have a colonizer or a combination of the colonizer and the colonized, there is a great danger

that the colonizer will resort to racism. In many cases racism is a part of the colonizer-colonized myth, because it easily supports the myth. It becomes easy to say that people who are of the black race do not know how to walk properly, are like children and do not know how to cooperate, that they don't have any drive, but just like to live for the present with no sense of planning, no maturity. This kind of racism has become such a built-in part of the myth of the colonizer and the colonized that we do not even think of it as racism.[33]

Such diminutive attitudes and behaviors are inculcated in the minds of some whites and self-depreciating blacks and manifested in patterns of relational and psychological aversion. The cognitive processes of white racist thinking and some black thinking presumes the inherent mediocrity of black people. Devaluation is a psychological and cognitive process in which the mind is so conditioned to lowering or diminishing expectations about black people that it limits itself to *diminutive thinking*. The tendency, then, is to dismiss the African-Ameri can as intellectually and culturally inferior. Whatever African-Americans conceive and accomplish is never quite the standard of their Anglo American counterpart. There remains a process of devaluation that limits the possibilities and potential of blacks.

Conversely, because some whites and blacks have so thoroughly brought into the myth of black inferiority, they must exalt a super black mind as a kind of messianic intellectual leviathan; a superhuman who becomes the paragon of Anglo intellectual virtue. These messiahs are often promulgated as the only legitimate intellects of the African-American experience. These superblack minds are celebrated as a kind of anomaly, freaks of nature, or aberrations from the norm. They are exalted as the model minds because they closely approximate Europeans' concept of intelligence.

The irony is that every major movement for black social change and freedom in America emanated from the "intellectually inferior" underclass that decided they had enough of racism and oppression. Every major movement has had an intelligentsia who did not necessarily meet the Anglo criteria of African superman. They were often people of the masses who had common sense and the courage to lead. The prevailing racial mythologies have not only created a specter of angst and psychological terror for African-Americans but have evolved those insidious cognitive techniques and processes that devalue the black mind and black thought, classifying them as being either inferior to whites, or if superior, abnormal.

Given these processes, then, there is small wonder that spirituality is so significant for blacks and accorded so much praise. Because the spirit and mind in Western thinking are viewed generally as separate entities, the presumption is that the spirit has no mind; that it is simply an amorphous, ethereal reality devoid of intellectual capacity. This is especially presumed in black spirituality, where spiritual practice is considered mindless. In the minds of some, black spirituality largely portends irrational thinking and signifies nothing but passion and raw emotion without the presence of intelligence and rational thinking.

According to racist thinking, African-American spirituality is devoid of intellect, cognitive capacity, and reflective consciousness. Because black people are mentally inferior they must resort to the practice of a primitive spirituality, where they shout, release, and dance out their faith and belief in God. The spirit manifested in African-American spirituality has no mind or rational basis but is simply an outlet for anguished outcries of a suffering people.

Devaluation is not simply a process of cognition that summarily reduces the value and worth of African-Americans but equally disparages the power and efficacy of their spirituality as an intelligent revitalizing soul force able to reverse the devastations of oppression.

64

At this juncture, let us add that another positive contribution of African-American spirituality is the manner in which it has helped black people dismiss the prevailing racist mythologies and encouraged them to cultivate cognitive and spiritual processes that empower them to value their own existence. This means that African-American spirituality is not simply emotive but equally cognitive and socially functional. It is the practice of mind, body, and spirit; those beliefs, dispositions, and behaviors that have instilled in African-Americans the capacity to realize, intelligize, and synthesize their existence into meaningful patterns of empowerment.

The "normative" cognitive processes that devalue and diminish black life, intelligence, and worth exemplified by white racism have been largely undermined and refuted by the praxis of spirituality. The spirit is not only omnipresent but omnipotent and omniscient, and the practice of that spirit's presence and power has been a chief cornerstone of African-American survival and freedom.

In speaking of African-American spirituality as it has influenced cognitive processes, we are referring to techniques of psychological *transcendence* and *inversion* that enable black people to invert and to go beyond the self-humanizing psychologizing induced by white racism. These psychological and spiritual techniques allow individuals to exceed the barriers and limitations imposed upon them. The mind, therefore, is always actualizing its larger cosmic-spiritual possibilities, reaching beyond the constraints and conditions created by racism into a larger purpose and reality. Being a child of God means that one's psychological analysis about who one is as a person will always be larger than the debilitating, social labels forced upon him. It means that my range of thinking about my personal worth will always exceed the social and racial limits that are designed to stagnate my potential. African-American spirituality has taught African-Americans to view and define themselves in much larger and more human categories than those fashioned by white racists. Therefore, I am because God is, and whatever I become will be, because God makes it possible.

The corroborative function of African-American spirituality is the reaffirmation of black intelligence, personhood, humanity, and self-worth amid conditions of psychological debilitation and racial mythologization and social dehumanization. African-American spirituality is congruous with the actualization of the black mind in positive response to white America, the realization and practice of existential, anthropological, and ethereal truth in face of psychological, relational, and cultural untruths. It is the positive reinforcement of black mind, body, and spirit in a society that has so fervently sought to devalue and delegitimize it through the perpetuation of debilitating racial mythologies.

Thus, we concur with L. Alex Swan's assertion that

> Freedom and liberation of African people must not and cannot be the function of the approval and legitimation of white people. Rather they are the function of the initiative, approval and legitimation of black people by black people.[34]

No other force in African-American life has worked to dispel the myths, to bolster black pride and strength, and to overcome the spiritual, physical, and psychological atrocities committed against African-Americans as the praxis of African-American spirituality. The preaching, teaching, testifying, resisting, shouting, praying, communing, making music, fellowshiping, and creating culture have consistently and assiduously corroborated the power, purpose, and value of African-American existence under conditions of depression, repression, and unmitigated oppression in America. That black faith and belief corroborates black life as valuable, positive, and meaningful is an important part of the function of African-American spirituality.[35]

The Transformative Function

Another important hallmark of African-American spirituality is the manner in which it is used as an instrument of personal and social transformation. Black people have always used their spirituality to transform themselves and their environment. If internal conditions could be positively changed, external conditions could also be changed by positive spiritual praxis.

The transformative function of black spirituality has given African-American people the spiritual wherewithal to adapt with dignity to a variety of conditions. The focus here is on the positive transformation of self and society. If the cruelties of slavery, racism, oppression, and, black self devaluation could not be transformed, the individual could be changed in response to those changeless conditions. A strong belief that God retains the ability to transform all of life is a foundational belief to the transformative function of African-American spiritual practice. Because God is the sovereign creator of the universe, God retains the capacity to change injustice to justice, oppression to freedom and hopelessness into hope. God also instills within the oppressed the adaptive mechanisms to change darkness into light and sorrow into joy.

The transformative capacities of black spirituality has thus empowered black people to adapt, confront, understand, reject, overcome, and finally transform their conditions into positive, creative culture of the soul, where God is the supreme instrument of change and black people are both the recipients and catalysts for change. There is then, a restlessness on the part of blacks in response to oppression, dehumanization of any source realities that prevent the realization of full personhood and potential. This restlessness anticipates that transformation of positive change will finally transpire on behalf of God's people. That African-Americans have been able to endure centuries of oppression and dehumanization attests to the transformative function of their spiritual praxis and belief. God gives his people the capacity to positively transform external and internal conditions. African-American spirituality has always valued the reality of positive transformation and instilled within African-Americans, beliefs, values, and practices that would facilitate such change in both their lives and the larger culture and society.

The Sacralative or Consecrative Function

To make sacred black lives that have been profaned, desecrated, and denigrated by the larger culture and society has been another strength of African-American spirituality. Whatever forces unleashed to further the desecration and demise of African-Americans have been stymied by African-American spiritual praxis. All life is sacred, even the lives of those who oppress, maim, and destroy others. There is then a sanctity of the created order. To oppress, destroy, dehumanize, and devalue other people on the basis of race, creed, belief, or orientation amounts to the desecration of human life. Because black spirituality has affirmed the sanctity of all life, life then must be preserved but not at the expense of one's soul. Christian spirituality, based on the teachings of Jesus, reveres the sanctity of life.

African spirituality has always valued life as sacred order in a sacred cosmos. Human life is the paramount expression of this sacred order. The denigration, desecration, and devaluation of life is simply an affront to God and a subversion of the spiritual values and beliefs which view life as sacred. Notwithstanding those segments of the African-American and Anglo communities, who have affirmed and practiced black denigration and devaluation, African-American people have largely escaped its devastating influences. There are black, white, and other people who hate black people and have devalued them completely to the point of desecration. But there are many black people and other people who having been exposed to such a culture have largely retained a sense of God and the sacred in the things of life. Having been continually humiliated and desecrated they have not become the desecrators in response. Instead they have chosen the way of God, affirming the sacredness of life. Their values and beliefs reinforce positive thinking and affirm the possibilities of God amid myriad disabilities. Because African-American spirituality has affirmed the moral imperatives of life as sacred, African Americans have largely maintained this view despite all attempts to diminish their self-worth and value. Notwithstanding the sacrilege of the larger culture forced upon them by slavery and racism, black people have largely kept the faith and fought the good fight against becoming thoroughly profane in response to the violation of others. What I mean here is that given the desecration of the larger culture to what they were constantly subjected, African Americans have still kept a firm belief in God that posits the sanctity of life and the self-worth and value of all human beings. African-American spirituality instilled within black people a sense of the sacred and has, thus enabled them to continually consecrate their love for God amid unholy and profane social conditions.

African-American spirituality has enabled black people to practice the sacred as a functional response to the constant desecration of black life by others. By affirming their self-worth as children of God and using God as an ultimate reference point for all behavior and belief, black people have actualized a strange and unique freedom that has set them uniquely apart. This freedom has embraced the idea of affirming what is holy amid unholy circumstances and valuing the purpose of God through the sanctity of the created order. To be free to affirm oneself as a sacred child of God in a society that has incessantly tried to destroy sanctity and self-worth is the quintessential freedom.

Chapter Five

Spirituality and Relational Freedom

A significant aspect of African-American spirituality in its application to human freedom, is the importance of establishing cooperative and harmonious relationships as the basis for the black *communitas*. African-American spirituality has provided the building blocks that make strong relationships and communities. At the heart of black freedom is the idea of the individual as a vital link in community with others. A. Okechukwu Ogbonnaya in his article, "Person as Community: An African Understanding of the Person as Intraphysic Community," observes:

> ...the community and its centers of vitality are the beginning and end of the individual. The person, too, is an integrating entity. The person has a principle of vitality as does the community. This center of vitality for the individual harmonizes and connects the community within the individual in the African worldview.[1]

Ogbonnaya refers to Kwesi Dickson to underscore the importance of community in the African worldview:

> A society (community) is in equilibrium when its customs are maintained, its goals attained and spirit powers given regular and adequate recognition. Members of society (community) are expected to live and act in such a way as to promote society's well being; to do otherwise is to court disaster, not only for the individual actor but for community as a whole.[2]

The individual is a community unto himself but participates in a larger community of other selves. For black people, being part of a larger social aggregate with a shared history of suffering, oppression, and liberation has given them a collective strength and vitality. Positive relationships are manifested in black relationships in general: the black family and extended family, and in the development of an ethos, where all blacks are actually and potentially viewed as persons of inestimable worth.

Evan M. Zuesse observes:

> Reality is not being, contrary to the prevalent Christian idea, but in relationship. The more one ties things together, the more power and transcendence, for power flows through relationships. The goal of life, then, is to maintain and join the cosmic web that holds and sustains all things and beings, to be part of the integral mutuality of things.[3]

Harmony and equilibrium are realized in the formation of positive relationships among black people through the practice of spirituality that affirms their ultimate sanctity and worth as persons. The corporate experience of black spiritual practice has historically provided a context in which the value of persons could be affirmed in the larger community. Not only does the context of black spirituality empower blacks to coexist harmoniously among themselves and others, but its corporate practice in the life of the church and the community provide opportunities for the establishment and strengthening of African-American community. Black people convening to praise God and celebrate life creates a basis for reinforcing group identity and communal solidarity. Spiritual praxis makes this possible.

Essential to the establishment of a vital community among black people is the development of a culture or ethos of positive relationships that facilitate the realization of human potential and establish a mutual network of collective soul force.

Building Positive Relationships in African-American Communities

Relationships promote a kinship or bond between black folk in America, where their humanity connects soul to soul and where belonging emerges among them. This kinship is created by the power of divine spirit, whose love and truth permeates the universe. As children of God, black people are essentially one people, seek oneness with all people notwithstanding their heterogeneity and diversity, and this union is the cornerstone of the African-American communities.

Hence, the practice of black spirituality within African-American communities underscores the importance of bonding and kinship, of sharing and caring, and relating to the other as the created of God. Without romanticizing or oversimplifying here, there remains within the ethos of African-American life a fundamental recognition that neither black life itself nor the community that sustains black life could exist without the power of God. This idea is the cornerstone of every relationship and action that establishes itself as community among African-American people. African-American spirituality teaches that each individual action has the potential for establishing community with others. Each act should be a divinely inspired activity that strengthens community through the cultivation of positive relationships.

The supremacy and power of God should be therefore internalized, vocalized, and behaviorized in every aspect of black life. Black spirituality embraces the belief that God is in charge of all things, and that the grace and power of God continues to help blacks overcome the barriers to self-unity and collective solidarity.

Invocation of the spirit in the affairs of community is important and is actualized not only through religious ceremonies and the practice of spiritual discipline in the corporate context but in every individual action that establishes black personhood as being authentically of God. Life is a continual process invoking increased awareness of God's promises, powers, and possibilities. The invocation and practice of God has thus been a liberating force in black life, for amid the forces of containment, conformity, and subjugation, the great task has been to merge oneself totally and unequivocally with the power of divine spirit as primary soul force.

Black spirituality diligently seeks to bridge the gap between creative divine presence and the reality and the power of the divine in their lives, and to use that awareness as a basis for empowerment and transformation. Thus the task of African-American spirituality is to sustain an awareness of God's presence, power, and work in black lives. This awareness of God's presence in every aspect of black life is an important dimension of black relationships and community, for the more blacks perpetuate and practice divine awareness in their lives each day, the more potential is actualized for human community. This awareness must also translate into constructive action and the positive transformation of self and community.

Thus, at the heart of the black community are relationships that rely upon the powers of a larger, beneficent spirit, who directs the paths and sets a positive course for black life and relationships so that human potential and wholeness can be realized even under adverse conditions.

We do not mean here that all black people coexist in blissful, sublime, problem-free communities. It simply means that given all the attempts to undermine communal, familial, and filial bonds by whites and others through racism, slavery, black-on-black crime, and other maladies, the creative practice of God and the assiduous invocation of spiritual reality as the ultimate guidepost for black life, behavior, and belief have become the prominent catalysts consolidating black communities. That black people have suffered at the hands of their adversaries and themselves for such a prolonged duration of time and have not experienced greater disaffection, disillusionment, and communal disintegration than they have attests to the miraculous power of God as a consoling, harmonizing, and healing force in African-American life. The fact that many black people can walk and talk, sing and praise, coexist in healthy relationships with themselves and with others or even boast of a life worthy of God is due largely to the practice of a liberating spirituality and a firm conviction in the power of God's spirit to make them whole. The power to overcome the impediments to community and strong human relationships among blacks is actualized through the incessant invocation of the spirit of God as a intercessory, liberating, and transforming force for African-American existence. Establishing positive relations is one of the important hallmarks of black spirituality as a consoling and consolidating force for human community.

Contiguity, Imminence, Catharsis, and Intimacy

Of cardinal concern to African-American communities are relationships forged through contiguity, imminence, catharsis, and intimacy. *Contiguity* is a term signifying physical and spatial closeness. To be contiguous to someone is to be near them physically, spiritually, and relationally. The realization of this reality in time and in space becomes an immediate possibility as a life-sustaining force. *Imminence* is recognizing

75

God's infinite possibilities of immediate transformative action within time and space. *Catharsis* is a process of releasing or transcending those anxieties, vexations, and aspirations of the mind, body, and soul as a remedy to unmitigated pain and suffering. *Intimacy* enables individuals to sustain vital bonds for the fulfillment of their personhood and humanity. People authenticate themselves relationally, spiritually, and communally as vital persons of worth through contiguity, imminence, catharsis, and intimacy.

Because African-American spirituality invariably embraces divine spirit or God as a reality that is always contiguous, imminent, cathartic, and intimate in relation to African Americans implies that these realities are equally significant in the formation and strengthening of African-American communities.

Relational Contiguity

A contiguity or relational closeness ideally exists between African Americans and is created in part by their perennial treatment as aliens or outsiders to the larger culture and society. While brought here on slave ships to build America's wealth, blacks were nevertheless unwanted intruders on foreign soil. As a result of this depreciation, black people established even closer ties as a means of reinforcing communal power, group identity, and solidarity, and also as a way of insulating themselves from the pain, persecution, and rejection by the larger society. Black spirituality, therefore, affirmed that because God is always near them in their struggles, suffering, and despair, contiguity between black people was necessary for strength and survival. Because blacks were outsiders, they had to rely upon the spirit of God to consolidate their interests as a community and to help them realize healing and wholeness amid social alienation and racial discrimination.

Contiguity creates strength and affirms the presence of a more powerful communal self among black people that cannot be achieved as mere individuals. This collective power of community creates a collective soul force that overrides and repudiates all efforts to destroy it.

The idea of contiguity is further established in its stress on the collective power and redemption of black people as a spiritual collective. Freedom, salvation, and liberation may transpire for blacks in much the same manner as they transpired for the Hebrews in Egypt. God not only works through the lives of individuals but the aggregate of an oppressed minority. Historically, the practice of African-American spirituality not only reinforced a concern for the consolidation of community through God's redemptive acts for blacks as a social aggregate but has substantiated the imperatives for maintaining close ties in community. The power and efficacy of black spirituality is realized in black people's collective actualization of personhood and strength as a social and spiritual collective. It is this realization of collective power, purpose, and strength that the need for human contiguity and continuity are further reinforced as a central matrix of African-American communities.

Some scholars argue that black contiguity was created by racism and segregation. Black people had to develop close kinship ties and bonds of solidarity out of necessity. While this may be true, a more important factor in shaping communal contiguity was the practice of spirituality in community, which not only established behaviors, ethical norms, and expectations in black communities but also emphasized the collective salvation and redemption of black people as a whole. Thus, African-American spirituality culminates corporately in the ceremonial and ritual practices of spiritual belief in community and in the promulgation of a theology that underscores their salvation and redemption as a spiritual collective.

Both segregation and the practice of black spirituality created a context for the emergence of black contiguity as a relational and communal form of black freedom. Contiguity as a vital form of communal and relational expression emerged not only from the patterns of social aversion among whites and blacks, but also through the dynamics, forms, and context of African-American spiritual praxis and belief.

Segregation created black contiguity through negative conditions and circumstances. Black spirituality overcame the devastations of segregation as a positive force for black unity and communal solidarity. While white people separated black people on the basis of color, God would unify, liberate, and strengthen them as a racially persecuted people on the basis of their color, spiritual belief and practice.

Freedom, therefore, is realized through the affirmation of communal and relational contiguity that negate black disintegration and fragmentation through the praxis of spiritual beliefs that embrace God's redemptive acts of black people in history.

Despite attempts by the larger culture to separate, alienate, fragment, and destroy the bonds of black community, black spirituality serves as a unifying, consolidating force for black contiguity. Despite prevailing belief, it is this relational and communal form of freedom that has ultimately created a unified sense of spiritual power in African-American communities.

Divine Imminence

If black contiguity engenders communal solidarity and strength in defiance to forces of disintegration and dissolution, divine imminence emphasizes the exigency of God's immediate intercession on behalf of the black community.

This intercession is prompted by black people's awareness of God's ability to immediate act on their behalf. It also means that black people are empowered to act for themselves as inspired by God.

Irradiating African-American existence is the idea that God is immediately present in all things, and that awareness of such presence is the guiding force for black existence.

The name, power, and reality of God are affirmed and invoked in all things. African-American spirituality teaches that such awareness is one of the most important aspects of black life. Affirming, acknowledging, and practicing imminence is the key to black people's understanding of their own capacities in relation to divine reality.

Permeating black existence and communities is the understanding that God is invariably and immediately at work binding, healing, nurturing, sustaining, and liberating relationships among the people. Sustained awareness of this divine activity on behalf of the black *communitas* is an important element of black consciousness, spirituality, and belief. God is the ultimate source of divine consciousness empowering African-Americans in their struggle for human dignity and survival. Divine imminence is essential to black communal empowerment, because it enables black people to name, define, and anticipate reality not in accordance with norms and predilections of adversaries but according to divine power and will.

In other words, at the heart of African-American communal life is a profound understanding of how, why, and when God works on behalf of the oppressed. Such awareness provides black people not only with knowledge of how God works within the continuum of historical time and human consciousness but provides them with the capacity to transcend and extend themselves beyond its material constraints. Divine imminence means that God has the first and last word in all affairs of African-American people.

God's activity provides a measure of personal freedom and autonomy that precludes complete control by the larger culture and society. So long as African-Americans rely upon divine imminence as an impetus for mediating awareness and strengthening the black community, adversaries can never wholly determine their destiny and worth. This freedom is manifested in the way black people view chronological time to their invocation of God's presence in their daily activities.

Thus, the *locus* of communal consciousness is manifested not only in the affinity African-Americans have for each other as an aggregate or group but also in the way their communities shape their ethos and culture around the awareness of God's immediate action in their lives. God will and does act on behalf of God's people, and the assurance that God will sustain such positive action on behalf of the suffering and oppressed is the basis of community identity and unity.

The idea of God's action on behalf of African-American people underscores the providence of God in orchestrating and liberating black people from the onus of dehumanization and oppression. James Cone asserts:

> What is it that keeps the community together when there are so many scares and hurts? What gives them the will and the courage to struggle in hope when so much in their environment says fighting is a waste of time? I think the only reasonable and objectionable explanation is to say that the people are right when they proclaim the presence of the divine power....[4]

God's providential action on behalf of black people is thus realized in community. The awareness of God's power is rooted in the divine capacity to act autonomously and hegemonically in community.

Divine imminence is recognizing that God is always near, will intercede on behalf of the black community, and will prompt them to transformative action for liberation and empowerment.

Earlier in this chapter we stated that the communal and relational forms of black freedom culminate in life that affirms the power of God's spirit as a unifying and liberating force for African-American people and that black spirituality teaches them to invoke the spirit's presence in all things. The fact that God will act in time and space on behalf of the oppressed in community is a further corroboration of the power of spiritual invocation as an aspect of divine reality.

By evoking an awareness of God's presence and power, African-Americans establish a context for communal history and empowerment through God's revelation and a framework for shaping a trajectory of belief and praxis that ensures their long-term liberation and survival.

Catharsis

Spiritual catharsis means purging the body, soul, mind, and feelings from all destructive impulses created by the realities of racism, adversity, and oppression. The spiritual effects are not only humanizing, but purifying. By releasing the pain and trauma caused by adversity and oppression, black people have transcended permanent spiritual, physical, and psychological denigration. Catharsis is an important part of individual and collective healing.

The experience of blacks in America necessitates the drive for personal belonging and unity in community. Communing to reaffirm a common purpose is an important aspect of African-American life. Because of alienation, segregation, and polarization among blacks and whites, the need to affirm and belong is an indispensable part of communal and relational formation and spiritual restoration.

Communing in the spirit of God, affirming the presence and power of God in black life not only establishes a context for personal freedom amid the strictures and constraints of a racist society but equally provides opportunities for releasing the dread and dross of living black in America.

Thus, spiritual, relational, and physical catharsis are actualized in African-American communities, where contiguity and divine imminence provide a foundation for shaping, solidifying, and addressing the ultimate concerns of black existence. Communing together provides emotional and psychological release from the myriad forces of dehumanization and oppression. Unifying, expressing, and affirming the power of God's spirit to shape and redeem lives is part of the collective catharsis of African-American people. The purpose of catharsis is to create an ethos that compels black people to express themselves freely and to reaffirm their power as a community in order to affect positive transformation of self, community, and society.

The horrors of slavery and other crimes committed against African-Americans have enabled them to develop a community in which they could come together to express and remedy their collective concerns. This creation of community that reinforced black identity, purpose, and solidarity became a redemptive force for the consolidation, liberation, and transformation of African-American people.

On the plantation, in camp fire meetings, at the hush harbor sessions and in black churches today, black people express and celebrate the powers of divine reality in relation to the harsh brutalities of daily experience. Collective soul force is expressed and actualized in community through various cathartic processes.

The praxis of African-American spirituality in early slave and later communities made possible the collective catharsis of community. It was here under the formation and practice of black spiritual belief that black people could commune in the spirit; interpret, celebrate, witness, lament, shout, sing, dance, pray, preach, plot escapes, and tell stories that reinforced their collective desire for social transformation and liberation. Blacks experienced this catharsis both in how black people expressed themselves about their plight and in the *content* and *forms* of the spirituality in which the catharsis was expressed. This element of releasing and freeing the spirit has always been a part of the ritual and ceremonial processes of African religion.

Again we affirm African-American spirituality not only as a unifying and cathartic force for black Americans by encouraging them to commune together to express their collective concerns spiritually but as a means of strengthening the power of community as liberating and healing force. Thus going to church to express spiritual belief collectively not only consistently provided relief to and gave voice to perpetually suffering black souls but instilled in them the capacity and strength to envision themselves as a unified force for communal transformation and empowerment. The practice and content of spirituality are thus the cornerstones to African-American freedom, for as long as black people had a place to express and to address their ultimate concerns as an aggregate community they could collectively affirm and reinforce their power to transform their collective plight.

Thus blacks not only came together to express their joys, pain, sorrow, and hope, but in so doing created a context for the perpetual affirmation of black communal and relational empowerment. They could freely, purely and cathartically express their creative soul force and true being in defiance and opposition to a system of racial domination and oppression. Expressing oneself openly and freely also translated into other areas of black life, but African-American spiritual practice gave blacks credence and power to be free in all phases of black life.

African-American spirituality provided black people with incentives to shout and release themselves collectively from the dross and dread of systemic racism. Providing this opportunity for black people to commune in the spirit and regularly express their collective concerns is a critical factor in laying the spiritual foundations of black consciousness, culture, and spirituality so essential to the formation of black belief, identity, and transformation.

An equally important aspect of black spirituality in this regard is the way it shaped expectations about relationships among black people as a basis for cultivating community. Numerous scholars such a E. Franklin Frazier, Herbert Gutman, Andrew Billingsley have cited the importance of the relational components of black family life.[5] While they differ in their beliefs about the state of black families in America, an important theme is the cohesive role of spirituality in helping black families surmount the perils of slavery, dehumanization, and oppression.

Numerous writers agree on the strength of black spirituality and religion in building and sustaining viable relationships among black people in black communities. They also stress the means by which spirituality has functioned as a cathartic and healing force for positive change in black life.

Having a place to spiritually express and release their sentiments and thoughts about life individually and collectively is an important aspect of African-American freedom and underscores the importance of people finding a place the for spiritual release. It means finding, affirming, and forging a community in which refuge, healing, solace, and harmony can be actualized in defiance to the alienation, dislocation, and dehumanization of the larger culture and society.

That black people have created a community in which the voice and power of their collective concerns could be expressed in ways that add meaning and vitality to their lives corroborates the power of black spirituality as a sustaining, transforming, and liberating force for black restoration, humanity, and survival in America. The cathartic power of black spirituality as a spiritual force for change and empowerment in African-American communities thus cannot be negated or obviated.

To release collectively the pain and hatred that anesthetizes black people against feeling for themselves and others is ultimately to liberate them from permanent antipathy as a state of individual and collective existence. That black people can sublimate their pain and anger into various forms of creative and collective expression without destroying themselves or their adversaries is an important dimension of African-American freedom. Blacks have largely learned to release their rage constructively through forms of spiritual, cultural, and physical catharsis rather than totally and destructively turning in on themselves and violating others.

To sublimate the different forms of psychological, physical, and relational pain into positive, creative, and resistant soul force is a salient dimension of the African-American paradigm of freedom. If black people did not have a place to express and actualize themselves, spiritually, they would have perished in complete unmitigated despair. Belief in God and the power of catharsis is an essential aspect of black freedom in America. As earlier stated in this work, it is freedom not to hate and freedom not to be filled with the venom of violent racial retribution. It is freedom to determine for oneself the most viable mode of existence that will preserve black humanity, dignity, sanity, and long-term survival. Spiritual catharsis in black communities has been a saving grace for African-American people, because it has enabled them to release their fears, problems, troubles, and sorrow freely within the context of a caring community.

Intimacy

Contiguity, imminence, and spiritual catharsis are invaluable modes of communal and relational freedom in African-American communities, as stated above. Intimacy, as a soul force for change and healing among African-Americans, is an equally important aspect.

African-American spiritual praxis recognizes the need for healing and intimacy among black people as a powerful force for healing both individually and communally. There is something about black people coming together; laughing together; praying together; singing together; touching, affirming, and embracing together that is a vital force for black freedom. Again we cannot underestimate the power of black spirituality as an organizing and liberating force for these collective concerns in community. Coming together intimately to pray, fellowship, love, and embrace each other has had significant value in preserving black humanity, sanity, and survival in America.

Intimacy provides a context for the black spirit's bonding, for soul force to activate communal solidarity. It affirms, corroborates, and heals those alienated from shattered bonds of kinship. Black people have always found it necessary to

85

establish individual and communal intimacy, thereby healing and realizing wholeness.

One of the most important factors cultivating intimacy in community is the idea that blacks have always had a complete intimacy with God that could not be destroyed by social, economic, and racial conditions. This intimacy has encouraged them to stay close to God and to not allow outside forces to polarize, sever, and ultimately destroy that divine relationship. Intimacy with God is essential to intimacy and healing within African-American communities. Developing a close relationship with God is the foundation to developing close relationships in community.

Touching, feeling, expressing, creating, and building are hallmarks of black communal formation and culture. The earliest manifestation of these patterns of behavior and interaction were not only actualized in the motherland as part of African spiritual and communal rituals but equally expressed in orbit of black plantation life, where black people intimately communed and co-existed, sharing their pain, hopes and aspirations for the future. We stated earlier that an important aspect of black humanity is the capacity to feel, empathize, and experience life and others soulfully and viscerally. The ability to feel and express the self is essential to freedom and wholeness. Black spirituality has always encouraged blacks to feel and express themselves wholly and unequivocally not only as a hallmark of their humanity, but in opposition to a culture and a people who had no feeling or compassion for them. To be free, then, is to be in touch with personal feelings and thoughts and to express them intimately as a vehicle for vitality and human wholeness.

Intimacy creates the context where individuals have the freedom to express themselves and be themselves freely and soulfully experiencing redemptive healing in community with others. Intimacy provides opportunities for healing with others and enables blacks to remain in touch with the core elements of their humanity.

Go into any African-American community in America, and you will see the need for intimacy played out in the rituals of black life. Touching, hugging, embracing, giving high or low fives are expressions of intimacy and solidarity. These modes of behavior presents a stark contrast to Anglo culture where people do not largely demonstrate such expressions of intimacy as openly or as ostensibly in corporate community.

Intimacy has been an important tool for black survival in America. Creating an ethos where the full expression of personal humanity is affirmed and actualized, it has become a significant aspect of black interaction and a positive norm of African-American communal life. Hugging affirms the personhood and humanity of the other. Touching acknowledges the humanity of the person as well as the spirit of God and the creative presence of God as a unifying life force. Intimacy is the nexus of interaction.

We must remember that an important component of the oppression, subjugation, and enslavement of African Americans is severance of those communal, familial, and personal bonds of "intimacy" that create vital personhood and vitality. Even the intimacy established on slave ships was broken with the separation of slaves arriving for auction in the market place.

Howard Thurman is again helpful:

> But it must be remembered that slavery was a dirty, sordid, inhuman business. When the slaves were taken from their homeland, the primary social unit was destroyed, and all immediate tribal and family ties were ruthlessly broken. This meant the severing of the link that gave the individual African a sense of *persona*. There is no more hapless victim than one who is cut off from family, from language, from one's roots. He is completely at the mercy of his environment, to be cowed, shaped, and molded by it at will.[6]

On the plantation the slave codes forbidding open expressions of intimacy or solidarity were brutally enforced. Black fami-

87

lies were thus under constant threat of having their intimacy destroyed by the removal, murder, or sale of a family member.

Except in matters of procreation, white overlords and masters virtually destroyed intimacy among the enslaved blacks. However, blacks expressed intimacy beyond the master's watchful eye. Again, the practice of African-American spiritual belief in those early slave communities is significant, because it created a context where black intimacy with God in the corporate worship and through other cultural idioms could be thoroughly and legitimately expressed. Intimacy occurred in the hush harbor and at the camp fire meetings, where blacks could "safely" commune together and express themselves in ways that reinforced their sanity, survival, and self-worth as human beings.

As outsiders brutalized by whites, the praxis of relational, spiritual, emotional, and physical intimacy created a climate for the realization of humanity, healing, health, and wholeness. To touch, to feel, to love, and to embrace through various means of social, sexual, and spiritual intercourse were essential to the survival of blacks in slavery. Without spiritual, relational, and physical intimacy blacks would hardly have survived the devastations of the plantation system. Slavery did not abolish the need for intimacy. It enabled black people to affirm themselves as genuine persons and realize human wholeness in a world that tore them away from their homeland, family, and virtually severed all tribal ties.

Even today African-American communities express the need for intimacy in various ways. Coming together as family, nation, church creates a collective vitality for African Americans. Bonding, healing, affirming, and celebrating the African-American community through intimacy is an important function of the liberation process. Without meaningful and personal intimacy and interaction, the vitality that makes for human contiguity and wholeness is seldom achieved.

The value of intimacy as an expression of black spirituality and black soul force exists not only in the kinship and family it generates through personal interaction but in the construction of closely knit communities through mutually life affirming interaction and dialogue.

An essential component of intimacy and community building among blacks is the opportunity to listen and to be listened to; to hear and to be heard. This is an important response to what Albert Camus calls the "unreasonable silence of the world."[7] In a world where blacks were seldom listened to or heard, dialogue with others creates avenues of intimacy that are requisite to healing the mind, body, and soul. An indispensable part of African-American freedom is finding places where blacks can actualize their humanness and sense of belonging and can intimately express and celebrate their feelings, thoughts, and aspirations for personal wholeness, wellness, and transformation.

The value of African-American spirituality then resides in the many ways it creates contexts for the collective dialogical processes where black people freely express themselves, speak and listen meaningfully with others and ultimately communicate with the God who creates a context for meaning that sets them free. Sharing, affirming, and communing are essential elements of the dialogical process integral to patterns of intimacy endemic to African-American communities. Listening is a way of affirming the importance of another.

What does intimacy have to do with black freedom? We stated earlier that because of the culture of racism and black exploitation, black people were largely denied the full, outward expression of true feelings as human beings. Invariably defined as less than human, black people were largely denied the outward ability to experience the full spectrum of emotions. The practice of intimacy allowed blacks to overcome those barriers to their own humanity, creating an ethos where the free, untrammeled expression of black life, feeling, and thought could be fully actualized. What they could not express openly, they could express privately thus obtaining a measure of compensation for the brutal culture of silence imposed upon them. Thus, emblematic of black life is the power of intimacy; the capacity to feel oneself and others, soulfully establishing and articulating patterns of meaningful interaction that facilitate human community.

Intimacy becomes a form of communal and relational freedom, because it allows for the realization of humanity in a world that has fervently tried to destroy it. The capacity to love and to be loved, that is, the ability to coexist in relationships where intimacy can be affirmed and maintained, is one of the highest expressions of human freedom in a culture and world that has assiduously sought to sever it.

The fact that black people can soulfully feel, love, express, and interact among themselves in a culture that insidiously tried to strip them of all remnants of a normal, civilized human existence is made possible by the practice of spiritual belief systems that value the necessity of communal coexistence and affirm the power of individuals to be, choose and express their paths of human vitality. Howard Thurman gives a telling account of this perception of black people's inability to feel.

> There was one old family for whom my grandmother had done laundry for years. The man owned the only hardware store in town. In the fall of the year, I would rake their leaves every afternoon and put them in a pile to burn. The family's little girl, four or five years old, waited for me to come from school to do my job. She was a lonely child and was not permitted to play with other kids in the neighborhood. She enjoyed following me around in the yard as I worked. One day, after I had made several piles for burning, she decided to play a game. Whenever she found a beautifully colored leaf, she would scatter the pile it was in to show it to me. Each time she did this, I would have to rake the leaves into a pile again. This grew bothersome, and it doubled my work. Finally, I said to her in some desperation, "Don't do that anymore because I don't

have time." She became very angry and continued to scatter the leaves. "I'm going to tell your father about this when he comes home," I said. With that, she lost her temper completely and, taking a straight pin out of her pinafore, jabbed me in the hand. I drew back in pain. "Have you lost your mind?" I asked. And she answered "Oh, Howard, that didn't hurt you! You can't feel!"[8]

Intimacy has provided black people with a means of insulating themselves from the vicissitudes and brutalities of black existence in America. Maintaining humanity is actualized through the gift of intimacy among African-American people.

To live and to let live, to heal and to be healed, these are part of the sacred striving of black life as actualized through the practice of black spirituality. At the core of spiritual belief is the sanctity of all human persons and the need to affirm others and to be affirmed. It is essential to the vitality and well being of the human soul. The social and relational rituals of African-American communal life have historically embraced the value of black life and created idioms of being and relating that have encouraged human fulfillment. African-American spirituality has always stressed the value and significance of such communal celebration as an expression of black humanity and black freedom.

Affirming intimacy amid the forces of depersonalization and dislocation is the pinnacle of personal and human freedom. The freedom to be is bound to the courage to act in ways that affect human wholeness for self and others. This great hallmark of African-American spirituality is the foundation to the formation, development, and continuation of the black *communitas*.

The African-American Family and Extended Family
Other relational and communal bastions of freedom are the black family and extended family. Although much has been

written about the dysfunctional nature of black families, it remains the primary bastion of strength, developing and solidifying the values, beliefs, and aspirations of black Americans.

The African-American family and extended family have insulated members from full dehumanization by the larger culture, for it is within the sacred circles of black family life that members can receive healing for pain, affirmation instead of denigration, and incentives to bond with people who really care for them

Eugene Genovese, Andrew Billingsley, Harriet Pipes McAdoo, Robert Staples, Wallace Charles Smith, Robert Hill, Willie Richardson, Herbert Gutman, and others have discussed the positive and redemptive dimensions of black families and basically refute the image of the black family as primarily dysfunctional, disintegrated, and disabling.[9] Joseph L. White terms this the "deficit-deficiency model" of black family life.[10]

The truth is that the African-American family has always been beset by myriad problems and difficulties since the time of slavery but has managed to overcome the perils of complete devastation because of the inculcation of spiritual belief systems that promote positive values and lifestyles.

While numerous scholars have cited the African-American church as the primary conservator and disseminator of spiritual values among African-American people, the black family and extended family have had equally definitive roles in conserving the values of black life.

Historically speaking, the black family has promoted spiritual empowerment. The bastion of black self-esteem and empowerment, it has given African-Americans a sense of dignity, power, and strength. In slavery, the family was an antidote to harsh brutalities of plantation life. In modern times it has provided an ethos of nurturing and sustenance that has given black people the power to face, confront, and overcome their plight.

Joseph L. White makes the following assertion:

> In the black experience tragedy is unavoidable. Resilience and revitalization of the human spirit are facilitated by the use of humor and by the knowledge that one is not alone, there are others who will bear witness to the profound sorrows of existence. Through this sharing, beginning with the extended family, we reach out and touch others and are connected to them in a series of interdependent relationships guided by a spirit of cooperation, mutual aid, beginning with extended family.... At the core of the Afro-American worldview with its emphasis on human vitality, openness to feelings, collective sharing, mutual support and creative synthesis is a holistic, humanistic conception of human beings and how they should relate to each other.[11]

Here White emphasizes the strength the "extended family model," that underscores the positive strengths of African-American families.

In the *Strengths of Black Families*, Robert Hill delineates the positive role African-American religion and spirituality in shaping and sustaining African-American families.[12] The role of black spirituality in fostering values and imparting strength to black families cannot be negated, for no other force in African-American life has imparted daily the imperatives for positive ethical behavior and reinforced a belief in God who creates, preserves, and transforms reality as the black family. The African-American family has been a monument of strength and a haven of freedom for African-American people.

Accordingly, it is precisely our contention that the black family has been a vehicle for freedom insofar as it has instilled positive values in black people and empowered them to live with dignity and humanity amid the trials and terrors of the American experience. We must remember the black family was virtually torn asunder during the Trans-Atlantic slave trade and was repeatedly dismembered on the plantation. That any semblance of familial normalcy could emerge for black people

93

attests to the work and power of God to solidify the family unit despite the constant attempts to destroy it. It is primarily because of the practice of spirituality and faith that black families were able to unite and to consolidate themselves against the uncertainties of plantation life and the terrors of continual oppression.

Virtually no other form of support other than religious beliefs and spiritual values sustained black families. One hallmark of the black family's strength that promotes freedom and signifies its strength is the ways in which it has taught family members to not hate their adversaries; but instead to live with dignity and to trust God. Thus, the black family has had a redemptive function in black life by encouraging black people to develop methods of survival that would not consume them in the vortex of racial hatred and despair.

In considering the history of the African-American family, we might affirm that a positive spiritual attribute has been its aversion to hatred and its capacity not to instill the same loathing of whites by blacks. It is my firm belief that black people, for the most part, have not been consumed by the fires of racism and hatred because black families as well as the black church have taught the ethic of Christian love and reconciliation. The black family in the practice of spirituality has been a bulwark of freedom by encouraging black people to choose more positive and proactive terms of response to their dehumanization and oppression.

Conversely, I am struck by the proliferation of hatred among some white Americans who have been taught by their families to abhor black people. This hatred has no rational foundation, for blacks have not stolen them from their homeland, brutalized their women, men, and children. Blacks have not created a system of racism and oppression where people are dehumanized and denigrated because of the color of their skin. After all that white people have done to blacks, it is blacks who should hate them and not the reverse. It is precisely because of the values, ethics, and spirituality instilled and practiced by black families that many blacks have avoided losing their souls in the incendiary fires of racial hatred and retaliatory violence in America. Christian spirituality and the teachings of Jesus have done much to reinforce non-hatred as a legitimate response to hatred.

Through the practice of spirituality the black family and extended family have created a culture and ethos where freedom from hatred, self-destruction, and other evils have flourished. Although both black and white people hate oppression, racism, and other *isms* that stifle human potential and the human right to be, it fair to say that most black people do not hate white people, and that this positive response to others despite their cruelty preserves the soul and humanity of African-Americans. It enables them to maintain some measure of moral authority amid the evils of racism and oppression. A people that can refuse to hate their adversaries in a culture and society that promulgates and glorifies such hatred are truly a free people.

African-American spirituality as a practice of freedom has encouraged African-Americans to cultivate other spiritual, cultural, and material resources that allow them to overcome, transcend, or negate the effects of dehumanization, devaluation, and oppression. Hating or destroying their enemies has never been a viable option in African-American spiritual belief systems. Instead of practicing these alternatives, creative energies were largely sublimated into developing a viable and personal relationship with God, cultivating black identity and self-esteem, by forging strong family ties and positive relationships, thereby creating a community in which all persons can ultimately belong and realize their humanity and potential. Let me say black people have hated the evil perpetrated against them by whites and the self-hatred of blacks created by a system of racial oppression. They resist any form of oppression, discrimination, and dehumanization and as victims have developed an affinity for those who also suffer from them. This does not mean that racial hatred of whites does not exist among black people. It only suggests that given the quantity and duration of racism black people have endured in America, it is a miracle that racial hatred is not more prevalent among them. The black church and the black family through the practice of black spirituality have helped many blacks rise above the cauldron of racial hatred. They have hated the evil without hating the evil doer.

Black spirituality thus has enabled the black family to become one of the empowerment resources in American society. It has enabled black Americans to surmount their plight and be resilient in their defiance all forms of oppression.

Thus African-Americans have always been a free people in that they have largely chosen moral responses to their oppression that have given them the ethical high ground. The violence of whites against blacks has not been turned in full measure upon whites. The various forms of systemic oppression and exploitation have not been visited back on whites in the same way they have been forced on blacks. The black family has enabled, encouraged, and nurtured the capacity of family members to confront and overcome the constraints of their human condition and to find ways of keeping intact their sanity and humanity as a people. Love, nurturing, empowerment, and compassion have been hallmarks of many black families. This has been one of the great achievements of African-American spirituality as a practice of human freedom and is something that is often obviated or negated as a central truth of black existence.

What has enabled the black family to survive some of the most inhuman conditions known to humankind? What resources did black families cultivate to fathom and overcome the difficulties of their existence? How could black people have survived four hundred years of racism, discrimination, lynching, oppression, dehumanization, denigration, and devaluation without completely losing their minds and souls, and committing mass suicide?

The spirituality of African-American people has made survival possible, because it gave African Americans a strength, power, and energy that could not be wholly diminished by others. Freedom, then, is the capacity to live with dignity under undignified conditions and the power to determine for oneself a positive course of action and destination amid incessantly negative alternatives. Because God is ultimately in charge of all things, God will have the final word in all their affairs. Black people will always be spiritually free, and the practice of spirituality within the black family has reinforced this value in African-American life.

The spiritual power and resourcefulness of the black family and extended family in instilling the values and praxis of freedom in African-American people must be thoroughly analyzed. It is the glue that has held America together and aided in the realization of her potential as a nation. That black people have not hated or destroyed white people or themselves on the level that many whites have hated or destroyed them is the gift of black spirituality to America.

We cannot possibly exhaust all the relational and communal forms of black freedom in one sitting. However, suffice it to say that the various modes of communication established through black oral culture and the role of the spirit of God in impacting the power and destiny of African-Americans is made more salient through the practice of African-American spirituality.

Black spirituality has thus, not only created the context in which the relational and communal forms of black freedom could be ritualized, reinforced, and practiced; it has instilled with black people a spiritual self-determination and sensibility that has enabled them to confront, transform, and transcend their social condition.

Freedom is actualized through those patterns of socialization, interaction, and communication that negate the values, assumptions, and a culture of hatred and repression employed by the larger society for black annihilation.

The fact that black families have created a culture allowing them to determine and to define the terms of their response to oppression and racism is also a manifestation of black freedom. The practice of African-American spirituality makes these patterns and configurations possible by emphasizing transcendence, creativity, ritualization, and relational empowerment among black people and thus allowing them to face, confront, and surmount the devastations of racism, dehumanization, and oppression.

Chapter Six

Spirituality and Institutional Freedom: The Gifts of the African-American Church

While it is not possible to delineate all the social and institutional forms of the African-American paradigm of freedom here, this work does affirm the African-American church as one of the most important institutions in history of African-American people. The black church has been the paramount harbinger of freedom; the curator of culture, equality, justice, and reconciliation among the black masses; and has, among all black institutions, maintained the greatest autonomy. To speak of institutional freedom appears to some to be an oxymoron. The truth is blacks have found a measure of freedom in the black church as an institution. The church has always wielded institutional power by shaping the values, culture, expectations, and aspirations of African-Americans.

The black church has taught perseverance; incited the establishment of a black Christian ethic; fueled the fight for freedom, and provided black people with a text, context, pretext, and subtext for the confirmation of human dignity among the people of God.

Many have maligned the role of the black church in acquiescing to the white power establishment. The black church has been criticized for not taking a more active role in the struggle for black freedom and empowerment; yet no other institution in African-American history has done more to organize, unify, preach, teach, reach, elevate, and enable black folk to freedom than the African-American church.

Invariably, the black church has been the citadel and bastion of the African-American struggle for freedom. James Cone makes the following observation:

> The black church was the creation of a black people whose daily existence was an encounter with the overwhelming and brutalizing reality of white power. For the slaves it was the sole source of personal identity and the sense of community.
>
> Though slaves had no social, economic, or political ties as a people, they had one humiliating factor in common—serfdom! The whole of their being was engulfed in a system intent on their annihilation as persons. The black church became the home base for revolution. Freedom and equality made up the central theme of the black church; and protest and action were the early marks of its uniqueness, as the black man fought for freedom.[1]

The black church is the principal institution of the African-American community where the praxis of spirituality and culture developed into transcendent forms of freedom that summarily translated into the social praxis of freedom. The black church has enabled black people to develop internal and external models of freedom. Those studies suggesting some disparity in the various forms of the black church have failed to consider the role of the black church in shaping black culture, consciousness, and belief. Those who defend the studies also fail to understand the role of the black church in preserving and transforming a spirituality of culture and a culture of spirituality among African-American people.

Lewis Baldwin affirms the role of the black spirituality and black culture in the consciousness of Martin Luther King, Jr., one of America's greatest prophets and church leaders. Baldwin is one of the first scholars to discuss the principal role of black culture in shaping the mind, philosophy, and theology of a major black theologian influenced by black spirituality who was simultaneously translating his spirituality into a social philosophy of human freedom.[2]

Many people have rightfully criticized the black church for its servile relationship with white society. James Cone relates the following:

> The black church thus lost its zeal for freedom in the midst of the new structures of white power. The rise of segregation and discrimination in the post-Civil War period softened its drive for equality. Black churches adopted, for the most part, the theology of the white missionaries and taught blacks to forget the present and look to the future. Some black ministers even urged blacks to adopt the morality of white society entirely, suggesting that entrance into the Kingdom of Heaven is dependent on obedience to the laws of white society.[3]

Despite this viewpoint, as Cone also affirms, the black church has not always been so abject and servile. While it has sometimes been more accommodating than liberating, it has still been a force for positive change in African-American life. Moreover, such accommodation is not invariably the result of oppressed people's failure of nerve or of their intrinsic desire to identify exclusively with their captors; rather it is a creative strategy emerging as an outgrowth to the creative practices of black culture and spirituality. African-Americans have not simply acquiesced with a system of oppression because they have had no choice. For some, such accommodation was born out of a fear of the white man and his power to destroy them. For others, it was simply a choice in a list of options made feasible through the praxis of culture and spirituality. In other words, because black culture and spirituality taught not only "acceptance" but transcendence of the white status quo and culture, and because creativity, innovation, improvisation, and transcendence have always been the catalysts of black culture, black people have always been compelled to choose between a variety of cultural alternatives.

Accomodating and adopting patterns of European culture is neither a sign of subservience nor of ignorance. Rather it is a manifestation of selective intelligence among a people who fathomed the foundations, necessities, and trajectories of human survival in a racist society.

The black church has always instilled in African-Americans the imperatives for establishing cultural fluency and intellectual vitality, and, contrary to the apologists of black history, the black church in every stage of its existence, has always been an institution of freedom for black Americans. In some previous interpretations, the tendency has been to limit and to define the black church according to the devaluations of historians. Certain historians, in their efforts to define American history, have categorized the black church according to the symmetry of their historical niches and definitions. The problem is that these historians have defined and limited the black church according to previously established historical paradigms and have failed to account for the initiative of the black church in cultivating its own spirituality and culture of freedom, that is, writing, interpreting, transforming, and transcending the historical epochs of these various historical periods.

As an institutional force for freedom, the black church equips African-Americans with the organizational apparatus that empowers them to navigate culturally and spiritually through the storms of the black experience.

As a social force for freedom, the black church empowers black people to create a spirituality of culture and a culture of spirituality that compels them to embrace, transcend, and ultimately transform the status quo. Gayraud Wilmore observes:

> The independent church movement among blacks, during the period of the slaves to have "a place of their own in which to worship God." But it was, in fact, a form of rebellion against the most accessible and vulnerable expression of white oppression and institutional racism in the nation: the American churches.[4]

Any serious analysis of the African-American church must consider how it has ingeniously equipped black people with spiritual and cultural survival skills along with developing a social philosophy of protest, which translates into movements for freedom and social change. Virtually every major movement for social freedom for African-Americans has been influenced by the black church. From slavery to Jim Crow to Civil Rights, the black church had been a powerful source for social change in America.

Even in examining the more militant black nationalist movements, we discover the presence and influence of the African American church. Malcolm X's father was a Baptist minister and other more radical leaders have been impacted by the African-American church. Frederick Douglass, Henry Highland Garnet, Henry McNeil Turner, Marcus Garvey, A. Philip Randolph, Malcolm X, Martin Luther King, Jr., Huey P. Newton, and even Louis Farrakhan have all been influenced by the black church. In speaking of the black church, we are not saying that it is some monolithic, homogenized institution devoid of diversity and variety. Some have argued that there is no black church in the singular sense of the term because there are too many variations within black culture and black religious beliefs and that the black church is really a confluence of different cultures, hermeneutics, and interpretations of the black religious experience. While this may be true, the black church remains representative of a uniform system of values and beliefs that facilitate the empowerment, transformation, and liberation of African-American people on various levels. Be they black Episcopalians, black Baptists, or black Methodists, black churches have a common goal that is to meliorate the spiritual, economic, social, political, and cultural realities of black people in America. Notwithstanding what has been said both pro and con about it, one cannot negate the black church as the most powerful force in the struggle for human dignity, justice, and freedom in American society.

While much of our discussion on the African-American paradigm of freedom has focused on how black spirituality has enabled blacks to develop those inner models of freedom, the black church has been decisive in facilitating the translation of culture and spirituality of freedom into viable social praxis. The principal focus of African-American spirituality has been the conservation of black soul force as an instrument of creativity, autonomy, and vitality. This soul force has not only shaped black identity and consciousness but, through the praxis of culture and spirituality, has created its own ethos of survival and freedom.

The capacity to create, interpret, and construct reality according to certain ethical and spiritual norms is an important element of the African-American paradigm of freedom. Even more significant is how it has adopted and translated those norms and practices into social movements for freedom. Thus African-American paradigm is not only cultural, but social and has been actualized through the teachings, preaching, and institutional gifts of the black church.

Institutional Freedom

The black church is virtually the only black institution that has been continually shaped and developed by African-Americans. In an outstanding study, Gayraud Wilmore offers a comprehensive view of the various aspects of freedom in relation to the development of the black church in America.[5]

While whites, particularly in large white denominations, have exercised certain forms of institutional control of the black church, the black church for the most part, evolved under its own aegis. The African-American church enabled African-Americans to create and cultivate their spirituality, welding them into a theology of empowerment and survival.

As *institution,* the black church models economic resourcefulness and development, vocational and educational empowerment through corporate praxis of spirituality. As *cultural force,* it has preserved the norms and forms of black culture institutionally. As *spiritual reality,* it has instilled in black people the imperatives for human dignity and freedom. It has buttressed them against the psychological and physical decimation of racism. Thus, the black church has simulated various processes of institutional empowerment as no other institution in American society. Black Americans have thus learned much about individual and familial empowerment by personifying and embodying in their personal lives the institutional processes learned from African-American churches.

For example, the principles of corporate economics have been embodied in the black church for many years. Black people may not have had a multiplicity of resources, but they could utilize the black church as means of institutionally facilitating their economic condition by learning various skills, trades, and tasks that would allow them to survive in the larger society. By observing how the black church has institutionally conducted itself in the conservation and utilization of minimal resources, many black people have learned how to cultivate and preserve those resources on a modicum of resources.

What the black church modeled institutionally was appropriated individually in the personal realm. If the black church could survive institutionally by the prudent stewardship of resources, why couldn't black families do the same thing individually?

The point here is that the qualities of corporate power the black church exemplifies institutionally have been personal lessons learned by blacks individually. The black church has thus been a force for institutional freedom, teaching African-Americans how to survive institutionally in a world of limited resources. By developing and simulating institutional norms and values, the black church remains a force for stability, maintenance, and positive transformation in African-American life. No other institution has afforded black Americans with such profound lessons on organizational skills and institutional empowerment as the African-American church.

L. Alex Swann, quoting Carrie Hunter, captures this description of the black church:

> The early Black church existed as the arena out of which all issues relating to Black life and existence could be addressed. It served as a social hall where Black people could fellowship and share talent. ... In addition to serving as the social hall in the Black community, the Black church was and is the chief property-owner, business activity supporter, and Black education promoter. Out of meager resources, during crucial periods in Black history, the Black church struggled to build educational institutions at all levels.[6]

This institutional empowerment has manifested itself through the cultivation of a culture of freedom. The black church is free to develop, shape, and transform itself according to its own sense of empowerment. That the church could retain a measure of personal autonomy and cultural hegemony in a white, racist society is a kind of freedom. White people could influence the black church, but black people would have the last word on determining its own future by building and shaping a community that would articulate and conserve the best interests of African-Americans.

The Black Church and Black Culture

As stated earlier in this work, black culture and black spirituality are the twin engines of the African-American paradigm of freedom. The black church has been created the refuge where black culture and spirituality could freely flourish. It was here within its hallowed halls that African Americans could create and express their soul force spiritually and culturally. L. Alex Swann again reminds us:

> The oppressed and powerless could not survive if they did not develop an ability to understand, manage, and endure suffering. It is not an acceptance of suffering but a way of perceiving one's position in relation to the social order and what is necessary to develop character and personality of endurance. The black church has assisted blacks in the process of character and personality development.[7]

Out of the suffering and chaos of black life, the African-American church became not only a *refuge* and *hospitality center* for the oppressed, but the creative and cultural life center that empowered black people to translate that suffering into creative acts of positive change. The effects of suffering could be transformed into a culture and spirituality that promoted and affirmed the imperatives of human freedom. By providing a context in which blacks could freely express their joy, sorrow, tribulation, and despair and be reaffirmed as persons of value and worth, the black church encouraged African-Americans to individually and collectively transcend the constraints of their condition.

The genesis of the African-American freedom, as previously stated, occurred before the black church was formally

107

institutionalized, Camp fire and hush harbor meetings, as previously stated, provided black slaves with opportunities to shape the chaos of reality through cultural and spiritual expression.

The institutionalized black church has continued to be a cultural center, where free expression, creativity, improvisation, innovation, spontaneity, and celebration of soul force is cultivated as an instrument of human freedom. If black people were free to worship, praise, and express themselves culturally and spiritually, they could be encouraged socially to forge their own reality, live on their own terms, and actualize a personal freedom that could promote survival, sanity, and vitality.

To fathom black culture we must understand the role of the black church in preserving, simulating, and developing those cultural and spiritual norms that influence the practice of black freedom. Being free to create a spirituality of culture and a culture of spirituality has profound implications for freedom in a social and political context. Invariably, the freedom actualized in the praxis of culture and spirituality must translate into freedom in the social realm.

It does not suffice, then, for black people simply to be culturally and spiritually free in church on Sunday morning, for the simulation and praxis of such freedom must find social and external expression in the larger society. Historically, we have seen how movements for social change have been spawned, ignited, or influenced by the black church, and this is largely due to its genius in cultivating the ethos and norms that make free, soul force expression necessary in the personal realm while providing a rationale for translating that expression as protest in the social realm.

The way a black singer interprets and sings a song is cultural freedom. The way an audience receives and feels the expression of soul in the black church is cultural freedom - actualized in the way it subliminally and consciously shapes the social, cultural, and spiritual expectations of black people in relation to themselves, their oppressors, and the larger society. So what occurs in the creation of culture in the black church is not simply an alternative or oppositional way of expressing oneself but a means of shaping culture, society, values, and expectations of life in God in the larger social arena.

If the black church is one of the few places where black people are truly free to express their feelings, it inherently provides the context and motivation in which those feelings must be translated into external reality. If black people can shout on Sunday morning about how good God has been, they can shout in protest about the evils and injustices in society.

Thus, the creation and cultivation of a soul force spirituality of culture and a culture of spirituality has profound implications for the struggle of freedom, justice, and equality in the social realm. However, without oversimplifying, we might say that the most prominent dimensions of the African-American paradigm of freedom suggest that cultural and spiritual freedom are the essential precursors of social and political freedom.

Essentially, there are two types of freedom. As noted in earlier chapters, (i) freedom that is external, social, political, and realized as a collective social reality and (ii) freedom that is internal, spiritual, and actualized inwardly. While both types of freedom are important in the African-American experience, the black church has primarily stressed the value of spiritual freedom as a foundation for social and political freedom. Where social and political freedom has been largely denied, blacks have cultivated a freedom that cultivates inner strength and power which allows them to confront and overcome social conditions. The African-American church has thus influenced every significant movement for black freedom in America. It is the creation, preservation, and development of black culture, however, that enables the black church to be such a powerful force for human freedom in American society.

The Practice of Nonviolence

One of the great gifts of the black church has been its teachings and urging African-Americans to live with dignity and to resist subjugation, dehumanization, domestication, and domination in all of its detrimental forms. More importantly, the black church has instilled within black people the capacity to survive and thrive in the midst of dehumanizing conditions. Perhaps one of the most significant achievements of the black church is the way it has empowered black people to realize their potential by establishing a mode of defense to racism and oppression that would not allow them to ultimately submit to its tyrannies nor endorse violence as a conventional response to white violence. That black people have been able to live in love, coexist nonviolently, even respectfully, with whites and other adversaries attests to the redemptive power of love and grace imparted through the practice of African-American Christian spirituality.

We stated earlier that given all the atrocities black people have endured, the fact that they have not lost their sanity nor developed *en masse* a pathological hatred towards white people, or sought mass retaliation for continual racism and oppression symbolizes the liberating power of African-American spirituality and the black church. Freedom from hatred, self-destruction, and violence as a legitimate response to oppression is one of the greatest assets of African-American spirituality. That black people can live with dignity in relation to those who have never repented of their atrocities and sins is not only remarkable but miraculous. The black church has never openly endorsed violence as a response to oppression.

Many have criticized the teachings of the black church on nonviolence by calling them accommodationist. The argument is that black people have conducted themselves in this manner because they lack of courage, nerve, or backbone in facing their adversaries. While some of this may be true, the fact is that many black people have chosen this course as an alternative to a culture of hatred and discrimination. By living largely in a conciliatory, nonviolent mode in response to oppression, blacks have chosen again the moral high ground. Thus, black people have not allowed their adversaries to dictate the terms and conditions of their response to oppression. The black church and African-American spirituality have done much to instill this ethic as a means of empowering black people to actualize their potential as full human beings.

Thus, living nonviolently in a violent society is a form of spiritual and social freedom. Living with compassion and empathy in a culture of dispassion, hatred, and apathy, especially in regard to black people, is living free of consuming hatred. It is choosing the mode of response that will facilitate the sanctity of life and respect for God's creation.

Perhaps Martin Luther King, Jr. is the person who best epitomizes the nonviolent teachings of the African-American church. While many people ascribe the foundation to King's nonviolent stance to Ghandian Satyagraha, his thought was influenced more by the creative soul force of the black church, the teachings of Jesus, and African-American spiritual praxis. Lewis Baldwin has correctly observed that it is the roots of black culture that had the most decisive influence on King's social philosophy.[8] Ghandian Satyagraha merely reinforced a nonviolent theology that had always been taught in the African-American church, particularly in the American south.

King simply translated into the social realm the beliefs that black people had been practicing *en masse* in relation to whites since their genesis of America. The practice of nonviolence was not a new mode of existence for blacks; it had always been part of the essential teachings of black Christian religion and black Christian spirituality. The same creative soul force that fuels the creation of culture as an expression of black freedom is the same creative soul force fueling nonviolent movements for change. At the heart of nonviolence is the belief that all people are inherently children of God, and that each individual should have the freedom to determine a redemptive course of action that will ensure freedom and vitality of the human community.

The nonviolence of King and Christian leaders in general and various black liberation movements emerged from the praxis of black spirituality and the teachings of the black church. That King ostensibly utilized Ghandi as a source for developing the collective strategies of nonviolence should not overshadow the role of black spirituality in shaping his nonviolent beliefs. At the heart of nonviolence are spiritual principles, which honor God and affirm soul force and love as redemptive forces in history.

That the black church would teach nonviolence in a culture of unmitigated violence is not because of cowardice on the part of African-American people. Religious ideals of humanity, justice, and freedom also inspired numerous violent slave revolts. African-Americans have largely chosen nonviolence as a means of consciously defying the violence and inhumanity of the larger culture and a means of preserving the humanity, sanctity, and self-worth of blacks in relation to themselves and their oppressors. Nonviolence means dealing from a position of moral, spiritual, and physical strength. For black people to coexist in America with a modicum of hatred and nonviolence towards whites who have not largely repented of their sins of violence and racism is a testimony to the redemptive power of God to renew and liberate black people in America. Choosing nonviolence was a deliberate attempt to fashion a mode of consciousness and being that would be in direct, unequivocal opposition to the violence of white Americans. Thus freedom to choose a path of sanity and harmony in response to the profanities and inhumanity of the larger society is rooted in African-American spiritual systems of belief.

The African-American Minister

In the struggle for African-American freedom, no one has been more influential in shaping black consciousness, black religious belief, and the social and political life of black people than the black minister. He or she is the symbol of freedom, vitality, and power.

The black minister has been maligned and criticized for taking an accommodationist stance in the struggle against white racism. Although belittled and besmirched for "selling out" the community and labeled hustler, pimp, and grab-bag theologian, in the final analysis, no one has done more to interpret, enable, nurture, and support the freedom of black people than the black minister. He has been the mainstay of black life, a harbinger of black hope, culture, and spirituality.

Vocationally, the black minister has become the symbol of freedom, interfacing with all segments of the black community. As priest, he heals the wounded and comforts the broken hearted. As prophet, he rightly rails against the evils and injustices of oppression and dehumanization and calls the powers into account. As teacher and preacher, he enthusiastically imparts the Word of God to the people of God. The black minister is lawyer, doctor, businessperson, banker, friend, brother, father and mother to those in need; an emblem of black freedom and the personification of the cultural and spiritual vitality of African-American people. Were it not for the black minister blacks would not have come thus far in the struggle for human dignity, freedom, and justice in America. However much the black minister has been excoriated and criticized, his or her role in empowering the black masses cannot be negated.

From the plantation to the present, the black minister's role has been as a *harbinger* of human freedom, *adjudicator* of black justice, *prospector* for black talents and resources, and *curator* of black culture. He or she has acted as *visionary, social* and *political activist, spiritual shaman, alchemist,* and *conjurer.* If one were to survey the black church's role in nurturing and cultivating black talent, the minister would occupy a paramount place.

In examining the struggle for social freedom historically, the black preacher has had an integral and definitive role in exhorting the black masses to actualize their greatest potential. A symbol of accommodation, liberation, transformation, and collective empowerment, the black minister is a major source of black culture, black consciousness, and black creativity.

Equally significant is the role of the black pastor as a kind of "spiritual ombudsman" for the African-American community. In the African-American paradigm of human freedom, his role has been primarily to serve as an interpreter, prophet, priest, healer, organizer, motivator, curator, transformer, spiritual shaman, and spiritual guide and as prospector of black human and material resources. As messenger of human freedom, his role is a vital element in the black church's empowerment of African-American people in American society.

Since the African-American church has had such an important role in shaping black consciousness and creativity by providing the ethos and context in which black culture and black spirituality have emerged in the praxis of human freedom, we must acknowledge the role of black ministers and preachers in the empowerment of African-American people.

More importantly, however, the black church has institutionally provided a refuge or context in which the practice of culture and spirituality could develop as creative forces for spiritual and social transformation in the African-American experience. The great gift of the black church is that it fosters the creation of internal liberation that has laid the foundation for social liberation. In this the black church has been particularly ingenious.

Examining its history, one begins to see how the black church has preserved through ritual, ceremony, institutional protocol, and spiritual teachings, the capacity of black people to actualize freedom under conditions of racism, domination, and dehumanization. That black people "safely" navigate through life's byways is due in part to the ability of the black church to instill within black people the capacity to think, create, embrace, and transcend the larger culture and status quo.

We have repeatedly stated the central thesis of this project: that the African-American paradigm of human freedom is predominantly cultural and spiritual, and that the way blacks developed and utilized culture and spirituality as creative soul force internally has a great impact on their quest for freedom in the social and political arena. But before we can fathom the necessities of social and political freedom, we must understand the African-American contribution in using culture and spirituality as instruments of creativity and transformation. While blacks have not always been socially free, because of racism, oppression, and other external constraints, they have been free to develop a culture and spirituality that has allowed them to transform the atrocities and absurdities of life into a meaningful, positive existence. It has allowed them to develop modes of response to oppression that has ensured their sanity and self worth as children of God.

The Black Church and the Hermeneutics of Freedom

Again, the African-American church has provided the hermeneutical, psychological, spiritual, ontological, cultural, vocational, educational, material, and institutional bridges between these two realms of human freedom. By encouraging black people to create culture by freely expressing and nurturing the spirit, the black church has inspired black people to practice human freedom both culturally and spiritually. Serving as vehicle for social transformation, the black church has coalesced the best of black freedom's internal modalities with its external social realities. Being free culturally and spiritually fosters the ethical imperatives for social freedom.

The truth here is that social freedom for African-Americans is a perpetual project. Spiritual freedom has largely been realized. The next step is the full realization of human freedom in every aspect of the personal and social realms.

Coalescing the two realms into a realizable framework for human existence has been no easy task, but since the black church has maintained relative institutional autonomy from whites, the development of these paradigms of freedom have been even more precocious.

Thus, not only has the integrity of black spiritual teachings and black culture been the bedrock of the black church, its institutional hegemony from complete control and domination by whites has been even more significant in helping black people cultivate models of freedom. The black church is the basic foundation for the amalgamation of these various human freedoms into a unique paradigm where spirituality dominates as both an organizing and totalizing force for positive change.

As stated in my earlier book, *African-American Church Growth*, the black church is the information center of African-American communities. By providing a living hermeneutic of spiritual vitality for the survival and transformation of African-American people, it has helped black people adapt to their condition and cope with their plight. These hermeneutics range from the way black people interpret the Bible for liberation purposes and the way they have utilized black culture and spirituality as founts for black creativity, to the way they have used worship as a forum for simulating black claims and aspirations for freedom.

In every aspect of ministry in the black church, the hermeneutics of black freedom are either suggested, portended, or actualized. Whether it is the Holy Ghost shout to release the dross, dread and pain of black existence or the black preacher's use of imagination to develop a sermon and take a text, it all exemplifies the power of the human spirit and creative soul force to transform the black condition. The black church has invariably challenged African-Americans to cultivate a spiritual hermeneutic that would enable them to transcend the vicissitudes of their social experience.

Furthermore, creative soul force in the life of the black church has enabled black people to develop internal models of human freedom through the use of black culture and spirituality. It has also enabled black people to develop external models of freedom, translating those forms into vehicles for social and political liberation. Thus the creative structures and modalities of black culture and spirituality are transformed into social forms of protest. The same presuppositions and motifs informing black people's understanding of God and helping them to realize their potential, actualizes the possibilities of freedom in the cultural and spiritual realm.

The African-American church is virtually the only institution affirming the values and imperatives of living out the cultural forms of freedom in the political and social arena. Although it has been criticized for not always providing blacks with the hermeneutical resources that incite them to more active resistance to oppression and tyranny, the African-American church has consistently sought to empower African-Americans to live out their freedom in various spiritual and social forms. For example, the emergence of the Civil Rights movement can be largely ascribed to the ability of the black church to translate spiritual freedom for all God's children into claims for social freedom. In order to realize a unified framework for freedom both socially and spiritually, it was imperative that black people learn that there were no hermeneutical disparities or ethical inconsistencies in their struggle for liberation. If it was wrong for pharaoh to enslave the Hebrews, it is wrong for whites to oppress blacks. The same creativity and soul force enabling them to construct a unique cultural and spiritual paradigm of human freedom could be translated ethically into a movement of social protest. The capacity of the black church to develop this hermeneutic of freedom is due in part to African creation cosmology and Christian spirituality which posits the universe as one and freedom as a power bequeathed by the Creator to the created at the genesis of creation. American constitutional culture,[9] particularly with its Bills of Rights which affirms the rights of all people to be free; and the amalgamation of a spirituality of culture and a culture of spirituality, that necessitates the use of black creativity and soul force as instruments of creating, human, and social transformation, are all important elements in the African-American concept of freedom.

Moreover, cultural, spiritual, and social freedoms are the most prominent themes in African-American life. That black people have overcome the cognitive, ethical, and practical barriers to these various forms of freedom can be attributed partially to the black church's ability to cultivate a living hermeneutic of human freedom that recognizes all forms of evil. The cultivation of a hermeneutic of freedom is based upon a realistic interpretation of the reality of race relations in America. Racism, oppression, dehumanization, domination, and subjugation are all social evils and the great task is to overcome such evil without becoming evil.

The hermeneutics of freedom rests, in part, upon the ethics of freedom, because it is important that blacks resist, defy, and surmount oppression without becoming oppressors themselves. The essential task is to realize freedom without destroying, dehumanizing, and humiliating others. While some would argue that becoming like oppressors should be the least of black peoples' worries in liberating themselves from the tyranny of racism and oppression, black spirituality has always affirmed that one could actualize oneself as free persons without becoming oppressors. It has enabled blacks to cultivate spiritual resources that help them face, confront, transform, and transcend evils of racism without largely becoming racists.

Some see this as a moral and ethical disadvantage arguing that this has been the bane of the African-American church. The issue here should not be whether black people become evil in the extirpation of evil in the society, but whether their struggle for liberation can be morally and spiritually justified as they seek to meliorate their condition. This is why many people see violence as a legitimate response to the violence of white racists. Violence is a means of destroying the violator and restoring human dignity to those who have been violated.

The point here is that the genius of the black church and black spirituality has been to provide a moral and theological framework for the struggle for black freedom without endorsing or sanctioning those methods of violence that could morally undermine the spiritual efficacy of the liberation movement. Notwithstanding all the atrocities, brutalities, abasement, scourge, dehumanization, and contempt blacks have suffered at the hands of some whites in America, they have still managed to cultivate a hermeneutic or response of freedom that has not diminished the moral precocity of their struggle for human justice. How could black people survive in racist America without becoming *en masse* racist? How could black people endure the social evils of America without wholly becoming socially evil? How could blacks experience lynchings without becoming lynchers, experience rape without becoming rapists, undergo annihilation without becoming wholesale mass murderers? As noted throughout this project, it is remarkable, even miraculous, that after all that blacks have endured they do not hold more malice, hatred, and outright loathing for their tormentors. This does not mean that blacks have not raped, pillaged, or murdered. It only means that in proportion to the violence done to them as a people they have largely been nonviolent in response to such brutality.

It is because the black church and black spirituality have encouraged black people to practice spiritual and cultural freedom through the creation of a culture of creativity and spirituality that sublimates, transforms, and ultimately transcends the constraints of racism, oppression, and dehumanization into a positive force for life that African Americans have been free to choose their terms of response to their condition. Because

God and creative soul force have been the central resources of African-American existence and because the black church has always nurtured these as essential to the struggle for human dignity and freedom, African-Americans, by and large, have resisted the temptation to do evil unto others as it has been done unto them.

This is why we consistently underscore the black church's role in the freedom of black people in America. It has created, nurtured, and sustained a culture where creative and resistant soul force could be activated as instruments for shaping the pain and chaos of black life into powerful litanies of hope, faith, and freedom. Because the African-American church has always stressed the importance of black people naming, defining, and transforming their existential reality into a positive force for liberation, its vital role in establishing cultural, spiritual, and even social freedom for African-Americans cannot be obviated.

Chapter Seven

Conclusion

We cannot possibly exhaust all of the salient aspects of African-American spirituality as a model of human freedom. What we have sought to provide here is insight into the ways black spirituality has shaped black consciousness and empowered the establishment and consolidation of the black *communitas.* The model of black spirituality proposed here is functional not contemplative or theoretical. Black spirituality has always had social and functional implications.

The African-American church as the primary institution preserving the creation, perpetuation, and practice of black spirituality thus has engendered the development of spiritual practices that invariably insulate blacks from complete subjugation and dehumanization by the larger culture. Throughout this project we have stated that freedom is not simply a social, political, or material goal; it also represents a full constellation of beliefs, attitudes, behaviors, and values that resist complete definition, domination, and devaluation by oppressors in whatever forms they appear. That African-Americans have survived slavery and some of the worst atrocities known to humankind suggests a model of freedom that has deliberately chosen alternative courses of belief and action to the predominant configurations of behavior and belief. To adopt the cruelties of the master would be to choose a path of existence fomented and dictated by the master himself. To choose and live according to a more humane model of existence exemplifies a freedom and self-determination often taken for granted.

African-American spirituality has always instilled within black people the capacity to confront, adapt, overcome, and transform reality through the creative actualization of soul force.

This soul force is manifested in the creation of jazz and blues to the walk, talk, and thought of black folk to the various forms of black resistance in the social, political and personal realms. The point here is that by enabling and nurturing creative and alternative modalities of consciousness, community behavior, and belief, African-American spirituality has engendered the formation of an ethos of consciousness and vitality among blacks that can never be wholly subject to, controlled by, or obliterated by themselves or their adversaries and oppressors. The central task of African-American spirituality has been to exemplify freedom of heart, mind, body, and soul in a society that fervently tried to keep heart, mind, body, and soul from being completely free through the reinforcement of mythologies, values, and beliefs that denigrated, devalued, and ultimately sought to destroy them.

The magnitude and mode of nonviolent responses to racism and the way African-Americans have creatively and spiritually responded to the absurdities of their condition all point to ideas of human freedom and dignity that depart from the trajectories of conventional ideas of freedom as simply external social goals and projects.

A central argument of this work is that social, racial, and political enslavement of black people did not mean that they were completely unfree. They managed to develop systems of value, meaning, and belief that reinforced their humanity, dignity, creativity, and power as a socially outcast people. They also created structures of consciousness, community, and culture that "insulated" them from complete consumption by the larger culture.

To create a culture of meaning in a culture of meaningless, and to create and reinforce values, ethics, beliefs, and behaviors that uniquely articulate, preserve, and transform black being and vitality is the mark of a spiritually free people. Blacks have been free to shape a distinct world of possibilities in a society of disabilities and dehumanization. Furthermore, to adapt and to appropriate those useful elements of the culture of their overlords and to integrate them meaningfully into their own systems of survival while maintaining a distinct identity and vitality is equally a hallmark of African-American freedom.

We have sought in this work and the previous one, *Soul Survivors*, to construct a paradigm of freedom that is unique to the African-American experience. No other models of freedom have delineated specifically how the praxis of black spirituality has created an ethos where cultural creativity has had such a vital role in shaping the consciousness and destiny of African-American people. We have tried to state in this project the ways in which African-American spirituality has created a functional model of freedom for blacks in America. This model is not contemplative as other models of spirituality, but is dynamic, active, and reflective. This project has also affirmed the manner in which black spirituality has compelled African-Americans to create a model of freedom that is primarily cultural and spiritual. Without a measure of cultural and spiritual freedom, blacks could not fully engage in the pursuit of social and political freedom. The central argument here is that spiritual freedom is the infrastructure of social and political freedom. It is precisely the pursuit and practice of such freedom in the spiritual realm that blacks could actualize themselves as free persons socially.

That African-Americans are still not fully free politically, socially, racially, and economically in American society has been a much delineated subject of discussion. What is needed is more discussion on how African-Americans have created a model of freedom through the creative, expressive, and resistant use of a culture and spirituality of soul force to establish meaning, consciousness, values, and community in a world of oppression, racism, and discrimination. Now needed is more discussion on the existence of this model and how African-Americans created it under such intense scrutiny, subjugation, and domination. That African-Americans are still here, living, acting, being, transforming, informing, and surviving with dignity, joy, vitality, and promises means that they have been free enough to exist, acting as God intended despite the intentions of their adversaries. That African-Americans are still here after all that has been committed against them means that they have had to be more than just imitators of their adversaries but fruitful creators of a consciousness and vitality that would ultimately fuel their recognition of themselves as persons of God and a people of power.

Notes

Chapter One

1. Dona Marimba Richards, *Let The Circle Be Unbroken: The Implications of African Spirituality in the Diaspora* (Trenton, N.J.: Red Sea Press, 1989), p. 36.
2. Ibid., p. 34.
3. Ibid., Richards, p. 34; Leonard Barrett, *Soul Force: African Heritage in Afro-American Religion* (Garden City, N.Y.: Anchor Press, 1974), p. 2.
4. Peter J. Paris, *The Spirituality of African Peoples* (Minneapolis, Minn.: Fortress Press, 1995), p. 22.
5. For further discussion, see Howard Thurman, *The Growing Edge* (Richmond, Ind.: Friends United Press, 1961). Thurman provides one of the first full explications by an African-American scholar of the cosmic and personal dimensions of spirituality. While Thurman's exegesis has implications for the spiritual life in general, his understanding emerges from the context of his experience as an African American.
6. Richards, p. 43.
7. Marimba Ani (Dona Richards), *Yurugu* (Trenton, N.J.: Africa World Press, 1994), p. xxviii.

Chapter Two

1. W. E. Abraham, *The Mind of Africa* (Chicago: University of Chicago Press, 1974), pp. 26-27.

2. See John Mbiti, *Introduction to African Religion* (Oxford: Heinemann International Press, 1975), pp. 32-36.
3. Ibid., p. 36.
4. See W.E. Abraham, p.20; Marimba Ani, *Yurugu* (Trenton, N.J.:Africa World Press, 1994), p. 92.
5. See Jean Jacques Rousseau, *The Social Contract* (New York: Washington Square Press, 1967), p. 7. While Rousseau closely approximates the African spiritual idea of human freedom, his discourse examines the reality of freedom in the context of society's power and privilege to confer these amenities on its citizens. In the African spiritual perspective, this freedom is never solely determined by the political and social order, or by the material or economic forces of history, but by God, nature, and spirit. These "rights" are given before the governing institutions of society were ever formed, and it is this idea that distinguishes African spiritual freedom from all others.
6. This idea of freedom, as it relates to the autonomy of nature and spirit, is decisively African in origin. There have been many theories delineated about the nature of freedom in Western society, beginning particularly with the Greeks and Romans. See Orlando Patterson, *Freedom and the Making of Western Culture* (New York: Harper-Collins Press, 1991). In tracing these origins, we must remember that the idea of freedom has not been ascribed its true parental source, i.e., Africa; it has been articulated solely from material, historical, and social bases. Patterson aptly distinguishes the three types of freedom: personal, sovereignal, and civic. He also affirms that such freedom is understood in relation to those rights, privileges, and amenities accorded by the governing institutions of society. However, long before these societies and subsequent ideas of freedom emerged, the African idea of freedom was rooted in a universal cosmology, which later translated into spiritual beliefs and practices whose remnants and vestiges are still visible today in various African and

African-American spiritual belief systems. Moreover, the social and materially based external freedoms, claimed as the exclusive properties of Western societies, cannot be fully understood without examining their African spiritual antecedents. Whatever analyses we offer about the types of freedom in the world, we must revert to this fundamental understanding of the role of nature and spirit in determining the nature of human freedom and the many forms in which they are manifested.

Chapter Three

1. Dona Marimba Richards, *Let the Circle Be Unbroken: The Implications of African Spirituality in the Diaspora* (Trenton, N.J.: Red Sea Press, 1989), p. 6.
2. Paulo Freire discusses co-intentionality in *Pedagogy of the Oppressed* (New York: Seabury Press, 1968), pp. 49-56.
3. Herbert Marcuse, *One Dimensional Man* (Boston: Beacon Press, 1964), pp. 84-91.
4. See Theophus Smith, *Conjuring Culture* (New York: Oxford University Press, 1994).
5. Malidome Patrice Somé, *Ritual, Power, Healing and Community* (Portland Oregon: Swan and Raven, 1993), p. 121.
6. Richards, pp. 31, 30.
7. John Blassingame, *The Slave Community* (New York: Oxford University Press, 1979), p. 134.
8. Victor Turner, *The Ritual Process: Structure and Anti-Structure* (New York: Cornell Paperback, 1969), pp. 94-165.
9. Malidome Patrice Somé, *Ritual, Power, Healing and Community* (Portland, Oregon.: Swan and Raven, 1993), pp. 120-127.
10. Monroe Fordham, *Major Themes in Northern Black Religious Thought 1800-1860* (New York: Exposition Press, 1975), p. 3.

11. For a discussion on liminality and ritual, see Victor Turner, *The Ritual Process: Structure and Anti-Structure* (New York: Cornell Paperback, 1969). See also Tom F. Driver, *The Magic of Ritual* (San Francisco: Harper Collins, 1991).

Chapter Four

1. Garth Baker-Fletcher, *Somebodyness: Martin Luther King, Jr., and the Theory of Dignity* (Minnesota: Fortress Press, 1993).
2. I qualify this statement with the word "some," for all too frequently generalizations about a group indict the aggregate. In describing the condition of racism, one oversimplification is to define all white people as racists, which is not only erroneous, but unfair to those whites who do not personify the description.
3. All too frequently we do not differentiate between racism and prejudice. Racism is the more systemic and institutional practice of racial bigotry and intolerance. It is reinforced by people with racial preferences and translated into the attitudes, behaviors, and folkways of the larger culture and society. Prejudice is simply individual dislike for a particular thing culminating in some form of discrimination. See Gordon Allport, *The Nature of Prejudice* (Reading: Addison-Wesley, 1987) and Joel Kovel, *White Racism: A Psychohistory* (New York: Columbia University Press, 1984). Both provide excellent analyses of these two phenomena.
4. Lawrence W. Levine, *Black Culture and Black Consciousness* (New York: Oxford University Press, 1977).
5. See Sterling Stuckey's *Slave Culture* (New York: Oxford University Press, 1987).
6. Henry Mitchell, *Black Belief* (New York: Harper and Row, 1975). Mitchell delineates the cultural implications of African-American spiritual and religious belief systems.

7. The implication here is that white masters did not overly concerned themselves with the behavior of blacks during the slaves' camp meetings and religious services. Knowing that slaves were coming together for "religious purposes" did not arouse as much suspicion as some other forms of communal gathering, where the purposes of such meetings were more obscure and thereby could be perceived as more subversive. Still, there was an ethos of scrutiny where the masters kept a watchful eye on their slaves.
8. Levine, p. 159.
9. V.P. Franklin, *Black Self-Determination: A Culture History of African American Resistance* (New York: Lawrence Hill Books), p. 75.
10. Robert Park, *Race and Culture* (New York: Free Press, 1950), p. 31.
11. We do not dispute that African-American culture had its beginnings in Africa and Europe. The point here is that the distinct formation of black culture in America took on communal significance with the practice of spirituality as an organizing and totalizing force for the indigenous black communities. Black spirituality is a parental source of black culture and community.
12. Akbar, Naim, "Mental Disorders Among African Americans," *Black Psychology*, ed. Reginald Jones (Berkley, Calif.: Cobb & Henry, 1991), pp. 343-349.
13. Riggins Earl, *Dark Symbols, Obscure Signs* (New York: Orbis, 1993), p. 161.
14. Ibid.
15. Herbert Aptheker, *American Negro Slave Revolts* (New York: International Publishers, 1943); Gayraud Wilmore, *Black Religion and Black Radicalism* (New York: Orbis, 1989).
16. Joseph White, *The Psychology of Blacks* (Englewood Cliffs N.J.: Prentice Hall, 1984), pp. 5, 31.

17. Personal Conversations with Joe James, 1989 (Detroit, Michigan).
18. John Blassingame, *The Slave Community* (Oxford: Oxford University Press, 1979), pp. 147-148.
19. Richards, *Let the Circle Be Unbroken: The Implications of African Spirituality* in the Diaspora (Trenton, N.J.: Red Sea Press, 1989), p. 215.
20. Alan Watts, *The Wisdom of Insecurity* (New York: Vintage Books, 1970), p. 26.
21. Gunnar Myrdal, *The Challenge of World Poverty* (New York: Vintage Books, 1970), p. 26.
22. Arnold Toynbee, *A Study of History* (London: Oxford University Press, 1961).
23. Kovel, *White Racism: A Psycho History* (New York: Columbia University Press, 1984), pp.13-14.
24. See Molefi Asante, *Malcolm X as Cultural Hero* (Trenton, N.J.: Africa World Press, 1993); Paulo Freire, *The Politics of Education* (Mass.: Bergin & Garvey, 1985).
25. Alfred North Whitehead, *Adventure of Ideas* (New York: MacMillan, 1961), p. 13.
26. Gunnar Myrdal, *The Challenge of World Poverty* (New York: Vintage Books, 1970), p. 26.
27. Michel Foucault, *Power/Knowledge: Selected Interviews & Other Writings, 1972-1977* (New York: Pantheon Books, 1980), pp. 131, 133.
28. Ibid., p. 133.
29. John McCall, *The Free and Colonized Person* (Denville, N.J.: Dimension Books, 1973), pp. 22-23.
30. Joseph Barndt, *Dismantling Racism* (Minneapolis: Augsburg, 1991), p. 61.
31. Kovel, *White Racism: A Psycho History*, pp. xxxiii-xli.
32. Barndt, p. 65.
33. McCall, pp. 16-17.
34. L. Alex Swan, *Survival and Progress* (Westport, Conn.: Greenwood Press, 1981), p. 31.

35. We stated earlier that all discussions regarding black freedom in America focus invariably on emancipation from external, political, and social power structures. Seldom does analysis underscore models of the internal, spiritual, and mental freedom that prevented complete enslavement and domestication of black people by whites. It is precisely this emphasis on the internal spiritual aspects of liberation through the practice of spirituality and the creation of black culture that makes the African-American paradigm of freedom unique.

Chapter Five

1. A. Okechuckwu Ogbonnaya, "Person As Community: An African Understanding of the Person As Intrapsychic Community" *Journal of Black Psychology*, Vol. 20, No. 1, February 1994), p. 79.
2. Ibid., p. 78.
3. Evan M. Zuesse, *Perseverance and Transmutation In Traditional Religion, African Religions in Contemporary Society*, ed. Jacob K. Olupona (New York: Paragon House, 1991), p. 173.
4. James Cone, *God of the Oppressed* (New York: Seabury Press, 1975), p. 122.
5. See E. Franklin Frazier, *The Negro Family in the United States* (Chicago: University of Chicago Press, 1973); Herbert G. Gutman, *The Black Family in Slavery and Freedom 1750-1925* (New York: Pantheon, 1976); Andrew Billingsley, *Climbing Jacob's Ladder: The Enduring Legacy of African American Families* (New York: Simon and Schuster, 1992) and *Black Families in White America* (Englewood, N.J.: Prentice Hall, 1968).
6. Howard Thurman, *With Head and Heart* (New York: Harcourt, Brace and Jovanovich, 1979), pp. 11-12.
7. Albert Camus, *The Myth of Sisyphus* (New York: Random House, 1955), p. 21.

8. Thuman op.cit *Head and Heart*, pp. 11-12.
9. See Eugene D. Genovese, "The Myth of the Absent Family," in *The Black Family Essays and Studies*, Third Edition, ed. Robert Staples (Belmont, Calif.: Wadsworth Publishing Co., 1986), pp. 29-34; Ibid., *The Black Family Past, Present & Future*, ed. Lee N. June (Grand Rapids, Mich.: Zondervan, 1991); Herbert Gutman, *The Black Family in Slavery 1750-1925* (New York: Pantheon Books, 1976); Andrew Billingsley, *Black Families in White America* (Englewood, N.J.: Prentice Hall, 1968); *Climbing Jacob's Ladder The Enduring Legacy of African American Families* (New York: Simon and Schuster, 1992); Wallace Charles Smith, *The Church in the Life of the Black Family* (Valley Forge, PA: Judson Press, 1988); Melvin Hitchens, Sr., *The Black Family and Marriage* (New York: Welstar Publications, 1993).
10. Joseph L. White, *The Psychology of Blacks* (Englewood Cliffs, N.J.: Prentice Hall, 1984).
11. Ibid., pp. 3-4.
12. Robert Hill, *The Strengths of Black Families* (New York: Emerson Hall, 1972).

Chapter Six

1. James Cone, *Black Theology and Black Power* (New York: Seabury Press, 1969), pp. 92, 94.
2. Lewis V. Baldwin, *There is a Balm in Gilead: The Cultural Roots of Dr. Martin Luther King, Jr.* (Minnesota: Fortress Press, 1991). Baldwin boldly traces the fundamental black roots of Martin Luther King's social and political philosophy and cites his sources without apology. The role of the black church in influencing the liturgy, history, philosophy, theology, community, and culture of African-Americans has not been explored precisely. Baldwin is one of the first scholars to develop a historical hermeneutic that employs black sources as a window

through which to examine and explain a great black thinker and activists using African-American cultural sources.

3. Cone, p. 105.
4. Gayraud S. Wilmore, *Black Religion and Black Radicalism* (New York. Orbis Books, 1989), p. 78.
5. Ibid., pp. 74-98.
6. L. Alex Swann, *Survival and Progress: The Afro-American Experience* (Westport, Conn.: Greenwood Press, 1981), pp. 128-129.
7. Ibid., p. 133.
8. See Baldwin, *There is a Balm in Gilead: The Cutural Roots of Dr. Martin Luther King, Jr.*
9. We contend that American constitutional culture has had a strong influence on black Americans' understanding of freedom in the American context. While many framers of the constitution were slaveholders and may have affirmed that blacks were inferior to whites, it does not negate the value or humanitarian principles contained in the American Constitution and Bill of Rights. In other words, although numerous whites ignored the Constitution relative to black people's constitutional rights, this did not preclude blacks from believing in its basic truths. Black Americans would always hold the larger society accountable for not living up to the claims of its Constitution. Thus, American constitutional culture has highly influenced black expectations regarding the promises and possibilities of social justice and civic freedom in both the spiritual and social domains.

Bibliography

Abraham, W.E. *The Mind of Africa.* Chicago: University of Chicago Press, 1962.

Akbar, Naim. *Breaking the Chains of Psychological Slavery.* Tallahassee, Fla.: Mind Productions, 1996.

————. "Mental Disorders Among African Americans," *Black Psychology*, ed. Reginald Jones. Berkeley, Calif.: Cobb & Henry Publishers, 1991.

Ani, Marimba. *Yurugu.* Trenton, N.J.: Africa World Press, 1994.

Aptheker, Herbert. *American Negro Slave Revolts.* New York: International Publishers, 1968.

Asante, Molefi. *Malcolm X As a Cultural Hero and Other Afro-Centric Essays.* Trenton, N.J.: Africa World Press, 1993.

Asante, Molefi and Asante, Kariamu. *African Culture: The Rhythms of Unity.* N.J.: Africa World Press, 1990.

Baer, Hans. *The Black Spiritual Movement: A Religious Response to Racism.* Knoxville: University of Tennessee, 1984.

Baldwin, James. *Go Tell it on the Mountain.* New York: Dell, 1953.

Baldwin, Lewis. *There is a Balm in Gilead.* Minn.: Fortress Press, 1991.

————. *To Make the Wounded Whole.* Minn.: Fortress Press, 1992.

Barndt, Joseph. *Dismantling Racism.* Minneapolis: Augsburg Press, 1991.

Bebey, Francis. *African Music: A People's Art.* New York: Lawrence Hill, 1975.

Bell, Bernard. *The Afro-American Novel and Its Tradition.* Amherst, Mass.: University of Massachusetts Press, 1987.

Beverly, Creigs, "Spirituality: Oft the Missing Link in African-American Mental Health." School of Social Work. Wayne State University, Detroit, Michigan, 1995.

Billingsley, Andrew. *Black Families in White America.* Englewood, N.J.: Prentice Hall, 1968.

Billingsley, Andrew. *Climbing Jacob's Ladder.* New York: Simon and Schuster, 1992.

Blackwell, James E. *The Black Community: Diversity and Unity.* New York: Harper Collins, 1991.

Blassingame, John. *The Slave Community.* Oxford: Oxford University Press, 1970.

Bonwick, James. *Egyptian Belief and Modern Thought.* London: African Publication Society, 1983.

Brewer, J. Mason. *American Negro Folklore.* New York: New York Times Quadrangle Books, 1968.

Brown, Sterling. *The Collected Poems.* ed. Michael S. Harper. Chicago: Tri-Quarterly, 1980.

Budge, E.A. Wallis. *From Fetishism to God in Ancient Egypt.* New York: Denver Books, 1988.

_____. *The Egyptian Book of the Dead.* New York: Bell Publishing, 1960.

Butcher, Margaret Just. *The Negro in American Culture.* New York: New American Library, 1956.

Charters, Samuel. *The Roots of the Blues.* New York: Perigee, 1981.

Chernof, John Miller. *African Rhythm and Sensibility.* Chicago: University of Chicago Press, 1979.

Cone, James. *God of the Oppressed.* New York: Seabury Press, 1975.

_____. *The Spiritual and the Blues.* New York: Seabury Press, 1972.

Dickson, Kwesi and Ellingsworth, Paul, eds. *Biblical Revelations and African Beliefs.* New York: Orbis Books, 1969.

Dixon, Christa K. *Negro Spirituals from Bible to Folk-Song.* Philadelphia: Fortress, 1976.

Driver, Tom. *The Magic of Ritual.* San Francisco: Harper Collins. 1991.

Ellison, Ralph. *The Invisible Man.* New York: Vintage Books, 1947.

Felder, Cain. *Troubling Biblical Waters.* New York: Orbis, 1989.

Evans, Anthony. *Are Blacks Spiritually Inferior to Whites?* Wenonah, New Jersey: Renaissance Publications, 1992.

Foucault, Michael. *Power/Knowledge, Selected Interviews and Other Writings 1972-1977.* New York: Panther Books, 1980.

Franklin, V.P. *Black Self-Determination.* New York: Lawrence Hill Books, 1992.

Frazier, E. Franklin. *Black Bourgeoisie.* New York: Free Press, 1957.

_____. *The Negro Family in the United States.* Chicago: University of Chicago Press, 1995.

Freire, Paulo. *The Politics of Education.* Massachusetts: Bergin & Garvey Publishers, 1985.

Gates, Henry Louis, Jr. *Figures in Black: Words, Signs, and the "Racial" Self.* New York: Oxford University Press, 1987.

_____. *The Signifying Monkey.* New York: Oxford University Press, 1988.

Gayle, Addison. *The Way of the New World: The Black Novel in America.* New York: Anchor Press, 1976.

Harding, Vincent. *There is a River: The Struggle for Freedom in America.* New York: Random House, 1983.

Hare, Nathan. *The Black Anglo Saxons.* Chicago: Third World Press, 1991.

Haskins, James and Butts, Hugh F. *Psychology of Black Language.* New York: Hippocrene Books, 1973.

Hughes, Langston and Bontemps, Arna, ed. *Book of Negro Folklore.* New York: Dodd Mead, 1958.

Hughes, Langston. *The Best of Simple.* New York: Hill and Wang, 1961.

Hutchinson, Earl Ofari. *The Assassination of the Black Male Image.* Los Angeles: Middle Passage Press, 1994.

Idowu, Bolanji E. *African Traditional Religion.* New York: Orbis Books, 1975.

Jones, Edward. *The Black Diaspora.* Seattle, Wash.: Edward Jones Associates, 1989.

Jones, Gayl. *Liberating Voices: Oral Traditions in African American Literature.* New York: Penguin Books, 1991.

Jones, Leroi. *Black Music.* New York: Quill, 1967.

————. *Blues People.* New York: Quill, 1963.

Jones, Reginald. *Black Psychology,* Third Edition. Berkley, Calif.: Cobb & Henry Publishers, 1991.

June, Lee N. *The Black Family: Past, Present, and Future.* Grand Rapids: Zondervan, 1991

Kardiner, Abram, M.D. and Ovesey, Lionel, M.D. *The Mark of Oppression.* New York: The World Publishing Company, 1969.

Kebede, Ashenafi. *The Roots of Black Music.* Florida: An Ethius Book, 1981

Kochman, Thomas. *Black and White Styles in Conflict.* Chicago: University of Chicago Press, 1981.

Kofsky, Frank. *Black Nationalism and the Revolution in Music.* New York: Pathfinder Press, 1970.

Kovel, Joel. *White Racism: A Psycho History.* New York: Columbia University Press, 1984.

Levine, Lawrence. *Black Culture and Consciousness.* Oxford: Oxford University, 1977.

Long, Charles. *Significations, Signs, Symbols and Images in the Interpretation of Religion.* Philadelphia: Fortress Press, 1986.

Mbiti, John. *African Religions and Philosophy.* New York: Anchor Books, 1970.

————. *Introduction to African Religion.* Oxford: Heinemann International Press, 1975.

McCall, John. *The Free and Colonized Person.* Denville, N.J.: Dimension Books, 1973.

Mellon, James, ed. *Bullwhip Days.* New York: Avon Books, 1988.

Mitchell, Henry. *Black Belief.* New York: Harper and Row, 1975.

Morrison, Toni. *Song of Solomon.* New York: New American Library, 1977.

Mydal, Gunnar. *The Challenge of World Poverty.* New York: Vintage Books, 1970.

Neal, Larry. *Visions of a Liberated Future.* New York: Thunder Mouths Press, 1989.

Nkeita, J.H. Kwabena. *The Music of Africa.* New York: W.W. Norton, 1974.

Nobles, Wade. *African Psychology.* Oakland, California: Black Family Institute, 1986.

Ogbonnaya, A. Okechukwu. *On Communication Divinity: An African-American Interpretation of the Trinity.* New York: Paragon House, 1994.

_____. "Person as Community: An African Understanding of the Person As an Intra-Psychic Community." *Journal of Black Psychology*, Vol. 20, No. 1. February, 1994.

Ogren, J. Kathy. *The Jazz Revolution.* New York: Oxford University Press, 1989.

Olupona, Jacob K. *African Traditional Religions in Contemporary Society.* New York: Paragon House, 1991

Park, Robert. *Race and Culture.* New York: Free Press, 1950.

Patterson, Orlando. *Freedom in the Making of Western Culture.* New York: Harper-Collins, 1991.

_____. *Slavery and Social Death.* Cambridge: Harvard University Press, 1982.

Raboteau, Albert J. *Slave Religion.* Oxford: Oxford University Press, 1978.

Richard, Dona Marimba. *Let the Circle be Unbroken.* Trenton, N.J.: Red Sea Press, 1989.

Rousseau, Jean Jacques. *The Social Contract and Discourse on the Origin of Inequality.* New York: Washington Square Books, 1967.

Rutstein, Nathan. *Healing Racism.* Springfield, Mass.: Whitcomb Publishers, 1993.

Smitherman, Geneva. *Talkin' and Testifyin': The Language of Black America.* Michigan: Wayne State University Press, 1977.

Smith, Wallace Charles. *The Church in the Life of the Black Family.* Valley Forge: Judson Press, 1988.

Somé, Malidome Patrice. *Ritual Power Healing and Community.* Portland, Ore.: Swan/Raven, 1993.

Southern, Eileen. *The Music of Black Americans.* Second Edition. New York: W.W. Norton, 1971.

Spencer, Jon Michael. *Protest and Praise Sacred Music of Black Religion.* Minneapolis, Minn.: Fortress, 1990.

Staples, Robert. *The Black Family.* Belmont, Calif.: Wadsworth, 1986.

Steams, Marshall. *The Story of Jazz.* New York: Oxford University Press, 1958.

Stewart, Carlyle Fielding, III. *African American Church Growth.* Nashville: Abingdon Press, 1994.

_____. *Soul Survivors: An African American Spirituality.* Louisville: Westminster John Knox, 1997.

_____. *Street Corner Theology.* Nashville: John Winston, 1996.

_____. *The Black Church: Paragon of Strength for African-American Families.* Spaulding Institute. Detroit, Michigan, February 23, 1993.

Stuckey, Sterling. *Slave Culture.* New York: Oxford University Press, 1987.

Swann, L. Alex. *Survival and Progress: The African-American Experience.* Westport, Conn.: Greenwood Press, 1981.

Taylor, Hycel B. II *African-American Revolt of the Spirit.* Illinois: Faith & Freedom Publication, 1996.

Thurman, Howard. "America in Search of a Soul." 1-20-1976.

_____. *Deep River and the Negro Spiritual Speaks of Life and Death.* Richmond, Ind.: Friends United Press, 1975.

_____. *Jesus and the Disinherited.* Richmond, Ind.: Friends United Press, 1949.

_____. *With Head and Heart.* New York: Harcourt, Brace Joranovich, 1979.

Turner, Victor. *The Ritual Process*. New York: Cornell Paperbacks, 1969.

Washington, Joseph R., Jr. *Black Religion*. Boston: Beacon Press, 1964.

Watts, Alan. *The Wisdom of Insecurity*. New York: Vintage-Panther Books, 1951,

West, Cornell. *Prophecy Deliverance*. Philadelphia: Westminster Press, 1982.

White, Joseph. *The Psychology of Blacks*. Englewood Cliffs, N.J.: Prentice Hall, 1984.

Whitehead, Alfred North. *Adventures of Ideas*. New York: MacMillian Company, 1961.

Wilmore, Gayraud. *Black Religion and Black Radicalism*. New York: Orbis Books, 1989.

Wilson, Sule Greg. *The Drummers Path*. Rochester, Vermont: Destiny Books, 1992.

Witvliet, Theo. *The Way of the Black Messiah*. Oak Park, Ill.: Meyer Stone Books, 1987.

Wood, Forrest. *The Arrogance of Faith*. New York: Knopf, 1990.

Wright, Richard. *Native Son*. New York: Harper and Row, 1940.

Biographical Index

Topical Index